The Seer & Healing

THE SEER GIFT AND THE MINISTRY OF HEALING

Fred Raynaud

Book 2, The Seer Series
CELI Publication

Fred Raynaud/The Seer & Healing/The Seer Series, Book 2
www.Seersgift.com

Book Layout ©2014 BookDesignTemplates.com
"Original and modified cover art by NaCDS and CoverDesignStudio.com"
Ordering Information:
Quantity sales. Special discounts are available on quantity purchases by corporations, associations, and others. For details, contact the "Special Sales Department" at our website.

The Seer & Healing/Fred Raynaud. —1st ed.
ISBN 978-0-9892811-8-8

Contents

Acknowledgement.. 9

Preface 11

Thy Kingdom Come 17

    The Kingdom... 18

    The Model for Team Prayer....................................... 28

Healing and the Kingdom... 31

    Healing is Part of the Kingdom................................. 32

    How did Jesus Heal? 39

Healing and Seeing... 55

    Illustrative Example... 61

Directional Seeing 69

    Seeing What to Do... 69

    Illustrative Examples 73

Healing in General... 79

    The Seer and Healing... 79

    Illustrative Example... 80

Inner Healing 87

Sozo 97

Visions, Dreams, and the Ministry of Sozo 99

Illustrative Examples 100

Healing of the Demonized 125

Foundational Truths..129

Heaven, Angels, and the Demonic 135

Angels 137

Holy Angels..140

Evil Angels..141

Confined Fallen Angels 142

Free evil angels..144

Shifting Atmospheres..146

What are Demons? 151

demons and Necromancy..154

Revelatory Insight...157

Dealing with demons..175

Deliverance..178

The effect of demonic oppression 180

Personal Preparation and the Deliverance Process...................181

My Story 185

Bibliography... 211

About the Author 213

To my daughter
Nicole Chae (Raynaud) Moore

*"Jesus answered and said to them, "Go and tell John
the things you have seen and heard: that the blind
see, the lame walk, the lepers are cleansed, the deaf
hear, the dead are raised, the poor have the gospel
preached to them."*

- Luke 7:22

On February 21, 1988, at 8:08 PM, my daughter, Nicole Chae Raynaud was born. Unlike her brother's 24 hour labor session, Nicole practically slid into this world. The event happened so fast we barley made it to the hospital. Literally, moments after our arrival, Nicole was in our arms. She was our second child with a gap of eight years between her and her older brother Jamisen. We nick-named her "beans" due to the "dos manos" burrito her mother consumed leading up to labor. To this day the effects of that burrito have governed the eating habits of my daughter, being a lover of Mexican food.

Nicole was a beautiful child, with long curly blond hair and vibrant green eyes her countenance radiated her inner kindness and lovely spirit. Nicole was my light and joy. Shortly after she was born we moved from Palm Springs California to Milwaukee Wisconsin, then to Orlando Florida, where I had gotten a job at Walt Disney World. She was two years old when we arrived in Orlando, and with free tickets to Disney, this was paradise for the kids. However, in six short months our paradise was about to change, or so we thought.

In the summer of 1990, Nicole was struck with a crippling decease. She had woken up crying, trying to tell us she couldn't walk, however her vocabulary was still under development. We tried to stand her up - but she collapsed in tears of pain.

In a total panic we rushed her to Orlando Medical Center. The doctors had no answers. I remember carefully handing her to the doctor, as she cried out, "Poppy... Poppy..." with tears streaming down her face and her little hands reaching out to me.

Tearfully, I watched as they took her away. My heart was breaking. Jan and I just clung to each other crying and sending prayers to heave. A short time latter the doctor returned and said they were transferring Nicole to Arnold Palmer's Children's Hospital. He said they weren't sure what was wrong.

The doctors ran a slew of tests. They finely told us that they needed to operate - they thought she might never walk again. After hearing that we fell apart. For hours and hours we prayed. My father came out from California and together we all waited to find out what was wrong. Days of diagnosis and nights of sleepless and prayer strung together like a tapestry.

The morning of the operation the specialist came and made an incision in her hip. He took a long syringe and drew fluid from inside her hip. To our complete amazement, the doctor returned completely blown away. He said, "I don't understand this, but we took a culture of the fluid in your daughter's hip and everything was dead. There is no need to operate. Her hip is going to be fine. We are going to put her on IV antibiotics. We need to keep her here for a week or so and continue to run tests."

In a healing miracle Jesus had answered our prayers and healed Nicole. The doctors first thought she have had muscular dystrophy, later they determined it was an extreme case Septic Arthritis. The infection within the joint can damage the cartilage permanently. Timely treatment of a hip infection in a child is important. Surgery is the only way to clean the hip joint of a child, because the hip is still growing, it is of utmost importance to protect the cartilage. Patients who sustain damage to their cartilage risk permanent hip joint damage. These patients may require hip replacement later in life if the damage to the cartilage is severe.

Yet due to the results of her test, surgery was averted and our little girl was ok! Thank you Jesus!!! We stayed at Arnold Palmer for 6 days, and returned home with an IV kit and lots of hugs and kisses.

God is a gracious and loving father who walks with us in all things.

I dedicate this book to my wonderful daughter Nicole Chae Raynaud-Moore who is now happily married to Wes Moore and mother of my amazing Granddaughter Anise Ella Moore. I Love you Beans!!!

Acknowledgement

There are several people I would like to acknowledge in the preparation of this book. Foremost I want to thank my wife Jan for putting up with my crazy schedule and supporting me while I got up in wee hours of the morning to take on this task.

Of course no writing effort would be complete without the diligence of a good Godly copyeditor, and Christy Jones, in spite of her tight schedule raising kids and preparing for various triathlons, heeded that call and helped me to hone my writing and stay focused on the subject at hand; thank you Christy, your work was a true blessing! Then there is my sister Jean, whose fine eye caught what we all missed, simple spelling and phraseology. Her attention to detail is incredible! Not to bad for a very bust grandmother! Love you Jean. Finely I would also like to thank my dear friend Leo Griego, for reading my early drafts and giving invaluable feedback and support.

Preface

"...If you diligently heed the voice of the Lord your God and do what is right in His sight, give ear to His commandments and keep all His statutes, I will put none of the diseases on you which I have brought on the Egyptians. For I am the Lord who heals you."

- Exodus 15:26

This book is the second book in the Seer Series. I volume one we explored the concept of the Seer gift and briefly looked at the language of visions and dreams. In this volume we will explore how the Seer gift functions in the life of the believer while ministering to those in need of healing. We will focus on three key areas of the healing ministry:

- Physical Healing or healing of the body
- Inner Healing or healing of the mind and soul
- Healing of the demonized

Our purpose is not to take an apologetical approach to healing. My assumption throughout this book is that God has poured out His Spirit upon His church for the advancement of the Kingdom of God and that all the Gifts of the Holy Spirit are alive and well in the Church today. Therefore, there is no need to expound on the theological background of the healing ministry.

For those interested in a deeper study of the healing ministry there are many wonderful books out there that outline this subject, a couple of my favorites being John Wimber's "Power Healing," published by Harper and Row, and the "Essential Guide to Healing" by Bill Johnson and Randy Clark, Chosen Books.

I will simply say that ministry to the sick is a demonstration of God's incredible love and heart towards people. It is a demonstration of God's power and the proclamation that the Kingdom of Heaven is at hand. Jesus is our ultimate role model. He is our example; compassion, love, and mission drove Him. He healed because someone asked Him to. He healed when someone asked Him because He always does what He sees His Father doing John 5:19. He heals today because He has never changed His mission or our great commission.

As to the Seer and Healing I have found many of the gifts blended together such as the word of knowledge, prophecy, burden bearing, discernment of spirits, and intersession, in the ministry of the Seer that deal specifically with healing. This would include both physical, inner healing, and the healing of the wounded soul.

These manifestations of the Spirit can take place in almost any kind of ministry form, whether it's a one on one situation, team ministry, pulpit ministry, intersession, counseling, or in the work place, the Holy Spirit will speak as the need arises if we are vessels open for his use. It is helpful then in understanding how these various gifts work through the Seer and how they relate to the Spirit's healing ministry.

If you are reading this series then the odds are you are a Spirit filled believer who is currently moving out in ministry operating through the gifts of the Holy Spirit. And, if you are like me you have not only witnessed God's touch with the miraculous but have also seen times when your prayers did not yield the intended results and you were left wondering why. There seems to be ebb and flow to the release of the Spirit's healing touch.

The sad thing is that many in the church fall back from the ministry of healing due to the lack of healing and answered prayer in their lives and or the lives of others. Yet, the truth is, we are called to partner with Christ, to destroy the works of the devil.

> *"He who sins is of the devil, for the devil has sinned from the beginning. For this purpose the Son of God was manifested, that He might destroy the works of the devil."*
>
> *- 1 John 3:8*

> *"And the God of peace will crush Satan under your feet shortly."*
>
> *- Romans 16:20*

> *"...not as Cain who was of the wicked one and murdered his brother. And why did he murder him? Because his works were evil and his brother's righteous."*
>
> *- 1 John 3:12*

In Christ our rule was restored on planet earth. We are ambassadors of the Kingdom of Heaven. We are His representatives on earth. We have obtained an inheritance (Ephesians 1:11-12).

> "In Him also we have obtained an inheritance, being predestined according to the purpose of Him who works all things according to the counsel of His will, that we who first trusted in Christ should be to the praise of His glory."

- Ephesians 1:11,12

We have been commissioned to take back the planet from the rule and reign of the enemy. This commission starts with prayer, and not simply a token prayer like saying grace before a meal, but radical prayer, where we engage the enemy with Holy empowerment and authority from Heaven.

The Purpose of this book is three fold:

- To encourage you to stay the course in being an ambassador of Christ.
- To help you live a life of believing God can and will use you not only to pray for the sick but work through you to heal.
- To help you understand how the seer gift operates in the life of the believer as they move out in praying for the sick and needy.

My hope is that by then end of this volume you will be equipped to pray at a more effective level with the understanding to see, listen, and hear what the Father is saying and do what He is showing you to do. This ability to listen is essential to functioning at a higher level of prayer. By knowing how to see, listen and hear, you will be better able to discern the actions and intents of the Holy Spirit in a given situation. The ministry of healing is meant for all Christians and is part of the good news that the Kingdom of God is near.

CHAPTER 1

Thy Kingdom Come

"Now it came to pass, as He was praying in a certain place, when He ceased, that one of His disciples said to Him, Lord, teach us to pray, as John also taught his disciples. So He said to them, When you pray, say:
Our Father in heaven, Hallowed be Your name. Your kingdom come. Your will be done, on earth as it is in heaven. ..."

- Luke 11:1-2"

"Then He called His twelve disciples together and gave them power and authority over all demons, and to cure diseases. He sent them to preach the kingdom of God and to heal the sick."

- Luke 9:1-2

The Kingdom

"After these things the Lord appointed seventy others also, and sent them two by two before His face into every city and place where He Himself was about to go. Then He said to them, The harvest truly is great, but the laborers are few; therefore pray the Lord of the harvest to send out laborers into His harvest.

Go your way; behold, I send you out as lambs among wolves. Carry neither money bag, knapsack, nor sandals; and greet no one along the road.

But whatever house you enter, first say, Peace to this house. And if a son of peace is there, your peace will rest on it; if not, it will return to you.

And remain in the same house, eating and drinking such things as they give, for the laborer is worthy of his wages. Do not go from house to house. Whatever city you enter, and they receive you, eat such things as are set before you.

And heal the sick there, and say to them, 'The kingdom of God has come near to you.'"

- Luke 10:1-9

Before we dive into the operation of visionary language in the midst of the healing ministry, I thought it best to layout some fundamental truths regarding the King we serve and His Kingdom.

I was saved in 1979 at a time when the church was experiencing tremendous revival. There were basically two streams of revival flowing at that time. The first stream was, what I will call, the Last Days Rapture stream proclaimed by such folks as Chuck Smith of Calvary Chapel Costa Mesa and Hal Lindsey, author of the Late Great Planet Earth. The second stream was, for lack of a better term, the Power Encounter stream ushered in by John Wimber of the Vineyard Christian Fellowship. Both moves were sweeping across the land with incredible speed. To the former, the Kingdom of God referred to the sudden return of Jesus Christ, His kingdom, and the pre-tribulation rapture of the church. For the latter, the Kingdom of God referred to the Kingdom, in the gospel sense of the word, as taught by Jesus Christ. Now this is an over simplification of the times but for the sake of expedience, it works for my purpose.

I was fortunate in three ways. First, the hand of God saved me, without any historical ties to church doctrine or religion which freed me to believe all that the scriptures said regarding the Good News and helped me to personally build a one on one relationship with my King that was not watered down by tradition. Secondly, my first church was Calvary Chapel of Costa Mesa under Chuck Smith. I was immersed in the word. With teachers like Chuck Missler, in depth bible study and worship became my passion. Calvary was the perfect place for being grounded in the word.

I was plunged in the eschatology of Calvary Chapel. In fact, I remember the day I was baptized, I drove my motorcycle to the cove in Newport Beach and was baptized in the ocean with about 300 other young people. Norwegian TV was there, filming the revival. I had made a t-shirt that said, "See you at the Rapture." Now, soaking wet I road my bike back home to tell Jan what had happened. I love the ministry of Calvary. Yet, during that season in my life, as I studied the scriptures and church history, I became disillusioned with the pre-tribulation theory of the rapture. I could not reconcile the persecution of the church throughout church history and the special treatment the church of the western world was expecting (read "Fox's Book of Martyrs" and dc Talk's "Jesus Freaks and the Voice of the Martyrs.") I also had trouble with the over emphasis of the Kingdom in the by-and-by, as opposed to the words of Christ when He taught us to pray, *"Thy Kingdom come, thy will be done, on earth as it is in Heaven."* This internal struggle lead me to the third reason I was I was fortunate, finding John Wimber and Vineyard Christian Fellowship.

It was 1981. That's when I discovered John Wimber at the Canyon High School in Yorba Linda. When I arrived it was shortly after that landmark day in Vineyard history – when on Mother's day, John Wimber asked Lonnie Frisbee to preach and at the end of his message he called all the kids under the age of 25 to come forward and hundreds came up – then he prayed "Come Holy Spirit" and the rest was history. God just fell on the place. That grace filled Mother's Day, was the beginning of the future Vineyard movement.

I found my home. I would spend half my time at Calvary Costa Mesa, learning the word, and half my time at John Wimber's church, just loving Jesus, worshiping, and soaking in the presence. They were meeting at the old Canyon High School in Anaheim Hills, worshiping on bleachers and seeking the face of Jesus. Then, in 1982, Calvary Chapel of Yorba Linda became the Anaheim Vineyard Christian Fellowship.

Vineyard was alive with the presence of God. You would simply walk in and the presence of the Holy Spirit was upon you

- Folks were getting healed left and right.
- The demonized were being set free everywhere.
- Miracles, signs and wonders were part of this new vibrant body of believers.
- The worship was alive with the breath of God.
- Kinship groups were training camps of fellowship were folks learned to practice the gifts of the Kingdom.

The non-pretentious, un-religious message and nature of John Wimber was refreshing for so many of us. We just wanted God to be God. John had a passion and a mission to train, equip, and deploy, and he had a vision to take the message of "**doing the stuff**" and "**everyone gets to play**" to the world. This naturally supernatural message was affecting denominations around the world.

Like Lonnie Frisbee before him, John was on fire for a personal relationship with the power and presence of Jesus Christ. John put into words everything I believed and was experiencing in my life. His passion for Jesus and his focus on Christians being authentic, filled, and "doing the stuff," was exactly what my DNA was crying out for. John Wimber developed a model of ministry that he had dubbed "naturally supernatural" and it reinforced in my heart the Lord's desire to live from a Kingdom mindset. His model took ministry off the platform and allowed all of us to participate in lending a hand to "**what the Father was doing.**"

John Wimber was a professional musician who played the Las Vegas circuit for 5 years. John later signed with the Righteous Brothers. When God gripped John in 1963, he was a "beer-guzzling, drug abusing pop musician, who was converted at the age of 29 while chain-smoking his way through a Quaker-led Bible Study.

One of my favorite stories of John's was when he recalled his first years as a believer. He became a voracious Bible reader and after weeks of reading about life changing miracles in the Bible and attending, what he called "boring" church services. John asked a lay leader at that "boring" church:

> *"When do we get to do the stuff? You know, the stuff here in the Bible; the stuff Jesus did, like healing the sick, raising the dead, healing the blind – stuff like that?"*
>
> *He was told that they didn't do that anymore – only what they did in their weekly services. John replied, "You mean I gave up drugs for that?"*

> \- John Wimber

John used to always say, "Everyone gets to play," which meant that all of us could participate in "doin' the stuff." It wasn't just for the pastors and preachers; it was for folks in the pews, folks like you and me. We soon learned that the "real meat was in the street" and Jesus was about to send all out and spawn a church growth movement that was simply remarkable. Everyone being allowed to do the stuff, the emphases on worship, and fellowship through "kinship" groups became part of the guiding foundation, hallmark, and marching orders of the Vineyard Movement in the early years.

John taught me that the most important thing in my life was intimacy with Jesus. That single core value has been my guiding pursuit for most my Christian life. I can say with full conviction that John was my true father in the faith, thank you John! John put into words the conflict that I was experiencing and the simplicity of the truth. John recalls his thinking on the Kingdom when he said:

> *"For the first twelve years of my Christian life, I gave little thought to the kingdom of God. My pastors and Bible teachers had taught that the kingdom would come at the second coming of Christ and, therefore, had little significance in our lives today...I find my neglect of the kingdom remarkable because it is so clearly at the center of Jesus' teaching ... I [now realize] that at the very heart of the gospel lies the kingdom of God, and that power for effective evangelism and discipleship relates directly to our understanding and experiencing the kingdom today."*

> - John Wimber

I like what John Bright had to say regarding the Kingdom of God:

> *"The gospel according to Mark begins the story of Jesus' ministry with these significant words" 'Jesus came into Galilee, preaching the gospel of God, saying, "The time is fulfilled, and the kingdom of God is at hand; repent, and believe in the gospel" (1:14—15). Mark thus*

> *makes it plain that the burden of Jesus'*
> *preaching was to announce the Kingdom of*
> *God; that was the central thing with which he*
> *was concerned. A reading of the teachings of*
> *Jesus as they are found in the Gospels only*
> *serves to bear this statement out. Everywhere*
> *the Kingdom of God is on his lips, and it is al-*
> *ways a matter of desperate importance."*

Perhaps, you have given little thought to the Kingdom of God. Maybe you were taught that the Kingdom of God was only something to be experienced when you die and go to heaven, or you, like many others, have not really thought about it in regards to your daily life and walk with Christ.

Yet the truth is, the Kingdom was central to the teachings of Christ. In fact, the phrase "Kingdom of God" or the "Kingdom of Heaven" appears 84 times in the gospels alone. How does this compare with other core Christian terms in the Gospels? Consider this: the "cross" appears 17 times, and the words "gospel" and "Good News" appear only 23 times.

In Luke 8:1-3 we read how Jesus went through every city and village, preaching and bringing the good news of the Kingdom of God.

> *"Now it came to pass, afterward, that He went*
> *through every city and village, preaching and*
> *bringing the glad tidings of the kingdom of*
> *God. And the twelve were with Him, and cer-*
> *tain women who had been healed of evil spir-*
> *its and infirmities—Mary called Magdalene,*
> *out of whom had come seven demons, and Jo-*
> *anna the wife of Chuza, Herod's steward, and*

Susanna, and many others who provided for
Him from their substance."

In this passage we see not only the words of the Kingdom proclaimed through preaching and teaching the demonstration of the Kingdom through the healing of the demonized. This is no better seen than when Jesus passes the baton to the twelve in Luke 9:1-2:

> *"Then He called His twelve disciples together*
> *and gave them power and authority over all*
> *demons, and to cure diseases. He sent them to*
> *preach the kingdom of God and to heal the*
> *sick."*

In this passage there is a clear connection to the preaching of the Kingdom of God and the release of power and authority to heal the sick. Some believe that this was some special impartation just for the twelve however, in Luke 10:1-9 we see a different story unfold:

> *"After these things the Lord appointed seventy*
> *others also, and sent them two by two before*
> *His face into every city and place where He*
> *Himself was about to go. Then He said to them,*
> *the harvest truly is great, but the laborers are*
> *few; therefore pray the Lord of the harvest to*
> *send out laborers into His harvest. Go your*
> *way; behold, I send you out as lambs among*
> *wolves.*
>
> *Carry neither money bag, knapsack, nor san-*
> *dals; and greet no one along the road. But*
> *whatever house you enter, first say, Peace to*
> *this house. And if a son of peace is there, your*
> *peace will rest on it; if not, it will return to you.*
> *And remain in the same house, eating and*

> *drinking such things as they give, for the la-*
> *borer is worthy of his wages. Do not go from*
> *house to house. Whatever city you enter, and*
> *they receive you, eat such things as are set be-*
> *fore you.*
>
> *And heal the sick there, and say to them, The*
> *kingdom of God has come near to you"*

John Wimber referred to Jesus as the "word worker" because he proclaimed the Kingdom of God and then demonstrated it through healing and deliverance. There is no better example of that than in Jesus' response to John the Baptist's question in Matthew 11, Jesus says:

> *"Go and tell John the things which you hear and see:*
> *The blind see and the lame walk; the lepers are*
> *cleansed and the deaf hear; the dead are raised up*
> *and the poor have the gospel preached to them."*

> *- Matthew 11:4-5*

These miracles, signs, and wonders were more than just a confirmation of Jesus' message. Healing and deliverance from demonic powers are tangible signs of the presence of the kingdom, just as much as salvation and the forgiveness of sins are the gifts God bestows upon us when we enter the Kingdom. We need to expect that these signs will follow those who believe when God's rule and reign is established in the here and now.

> *"And these signs will follow those who believe: In*
> *My name they will cast out demons; they will speak*
> *with new tongues; they will take up serpents; and if*
> *they drink anything deadly, it will by no means hurt*

*them; **they will lay hands on the sick, and they will recover.***"

- Mark 16:17-18

When His children release the Kingdom of God, folks get physically and spiritually better. Jesus "passed the baton" to His disciples: first to the twelve in Luke 9 and then to the seventy-two in Luke 10, now to all of the body of Christ. We are to do the things that Jesus did. In Acts 1:3 we read that that for forty days after the resurrection Jesus spoke to them all things pertaining to the Kingdom of God.

> *"He also presented Himself alive after His suffering by many infallible proofs, being seen by them during forty days and speaking of the things pertaining to the kingdom of God."*

In verses 4-8 we read:

> *"And being assembled together with them, He commanded them not to depart from Jerusalem, but to wait for the Promise of the Father, which, He said, you have heard from Me; for John truly baptized with water, but you shall be baptized with the Holy Spirit not many days from now.*
>
> *Therefore, when they had come together, they asked Him, saying, Lord, will You at this time restore the kingdom to Israel?*
>
> *And He said to them, It is not for you to know times or seasons which the Father has put in His own authority. But you shall receive power when the Holy Spirit has come upon you; and you shall be witnesses to Me in Jerusalem, and*

*in all Judea and Samaria, and to the end of the
earth"*

The Kingdom of God was central to the ministry of Jesus. His
desire to fill His children with power and pass on His authority is part of the Kingdom culture. He came to proclaim that
the rule of satan was over, and His Father's Kingdom was
established and advancing. Once we get this - that Jesus
came preaching the good news of the Kingdom of God, we
will be able to grasp more fully everything He taught and did
while He was on this earth. This is vital to understand. To be
effective as ministers of the gospel we not only need to be
hearers of the Word but doers of the Word - in power. The
following model will help you and your team, become affec-
tive in ministering to those in need.

The Model for Team Prayer

John Wimber sets out one of the best models that I have seen
for prayer-ministry in his book "Power Healing." John gives
us a five-step process that the prayer team should go
through while ministering to someone. I must point out that
it is recommended that three to no more than four people be
involved in team ministry. One person should take the lead
i.e. ask the questions, direct the prayer; this will cut back on
any confusion. The others should pray silently in their prayer language and listen to the Spirit for God for direction.

The first step in this five-step model is what John calls the
Interview. Here the person is asked - what do you need
prayer for? Where does it hurt? This is not a medical interview but a very practical time of probing. John tells us that

we should listen on two levels: the natural and the supernatural. On the natural level, we evaluate the answer through the filter of our biblical knowledge, what we know about the person, and our own experience in praying for similar problems. On the supernatural level, we listen to what the Spirit of God has to say about this hurt.

The second step is referred to as, making a diagnostic decision. It is here in this step that we identify and clarify the root of the person's problem. This is where we ask the Holy Spirit to give insight into the condition and root cause if any. This can come through words of knowledge or wisdom, prophetically, discernment of spirits. For the seer this information often comes through the vehicle of visions. This is also the time we learn what kind of prayer is needed to bring healing.

Step three, is referred to as, the prayer selection. At this point, we are agreeing with the perfect will of God. We are waiting for a green light, not only what to pray for but when the Lord is going to heal this person. There are many types of prayers. They include, according to John, the following:

- Prayers of petition
- Intercession
- Words of command
- Proclamation
- Prophecy

These prayers will take one of two roles. First, words directed towards God and secondly, words that we receive from God. These can be words such as commands spoken to a demon or the condition, a prophecy or proclamation, or pronouncement, or rebuke. At this point, you may also ask your team if they have anything to add.

John refers to step four as, the prayer of engagement. Here the question is answered - how are we doing? In this mode, we look for symptoms of the presence of the Holy Spirit upon the person being prayed for i.e. warmth or heat, tingling sensations, trembling or shaking, deeper breathing, eyes that flutter, laughing, sobbing, exuberant praise, and so forth. At this point, it is appropriate to ask questions. Do you feel anything right now? Has God shown you anything? This process will keep you in the flow of what God is doing. Questions will not disturb the ministry process.

The final step is post prayer direction. What does this person need to do to retain this healing? What should be done if the person is not healed? This is a very practical step and a time for you to ask God to solidify what he is doing in the person's heart. For a deeper understanding of team ministry healing, I recommend John's book highly.

To be effective in proclaiming the kingdom it is critical that we learn how to pray and the importance of team prayer ministry. Team is at the heart of being a member of the body of Christ. Only by engaging the enemy will we be able to the glory of His kingdom here on earth.

CHAPTER 2

Healing and the Kingdom

"Now when He was asked by the Pharisees when the kingdom of God would come, He answered them and said, the kingdom of God does not come with observation; nor will they say, See here! Or See there! For indeed, the kingdom of God is within you."

- Luke 17: 20-21

"Then Jesus answered and said to them, Most assuredly, I say to you, the Son can do nothing of Himself, but what He sees the Father do; for whatever He does, the Son also does in like manner. For the Father loves the Son, and shows Him all things that He Himself does; and He will show Him greater works than these, that you may marvel. For as the Father raises the dead and gives life to them, even so the Son gives life to whom He will"

- John 5:19-21

Healing is Part of the Kingdom

My first experience with healing happened in Canada shortly after Jan and I got married. We had moved from Huntington Beach and taken a trip to Vancouver, Canada, to open a restaurant at my cousin Jim's hotel in Whistler. Many incredible things happened up there on that mountain. I remember, during one snowstorm, a little boy came running into the hotel lobby, crying uncontrollably. Everyone in the bar came running out to see what was wrong. When I ran outside, I saw the boy standing over the body of a dead frozen dog, lying in the snow. A man, who also happened to be a doctor walked over and checked the dog's vitals – He confirmed it, the dog was dead. Now the boy was really weeping. I couldn't take it. My heart was breaking for that child – I ran over to the dog, placed my hands on it, and cried out to Jesus. Faith surged in my heart and I said, **"In the name of Jesus, get up!"**

Suddenly, the dog began to shiver, and then shake, and then it stood, shaking and running in circles. **God had raised it from the dead**. I was crying and laughing, the boy was crying and laughing, and the crowd just stood there amazed as this boy hugged his dog.

Now, here's the thing. Jesus intervened in a situation that many would think was too small or insignificant for His attention. After all, it's only a dog. However, that is not the case. Jesus was drawn by two elements, compassion and faith. These two elements were magnets for the Holy Spirit because they reflect the heart nature of the Father and glorify who He is.

The love nature of God is far greater than we can comprehend. What I love about this story is that the tears of a child, the faith of a young cook, and the frozen dead body of a boy's dog became a sign and a wonder to a crowd in a hotel bar. God is truly amazing, indeed (see Mark 16:17)!

I thank God I was a young Christian. The only model I had for such an event was what I read in scripture. I suspect that had I been around the church for a while and had been taught, like many others, that the wonders of Jesus were meant only for Him, in that time, and at that season, my faith would have fizzled out. On the contrary, the Jesus I read about, the Jesus I had come to know was the Jesus of the Gospels and His love heart spawned a fire in my heart that drove me to action, and to seek His faith. This event also set me on a path to understand God's heart towards healing. As a result, I found that I had many more questions than I had answers.

The biggest question was, is it God's will to always heal the sick? If healing is something God wants us to do and experience, then we ought to pray for the sick whenever we can. But if healing is not God's will, then praying for the sick is both pointless and wrong. It's pointless, because praying won't change what God decrees, and it's wrong because Jesus instructs us to pray according to the will of God.

As Christians, the primary way we determine the will of God is by the Scriptures. In the Bible, God reveals His plan for us and our actions and deeds to be accomplished here on earth. But some folks teach a radical view of God's sovereignty. The

Bible clearly teaches that God is sovereign and in control of His creation. However, when one takes the doctrine of God's sovereignty to an extreme, they assume that everything that happens in this world is also the will of God. As this thought process progresses they conclude that since nothing can happen that is outside of His will, then all sickness must be God's will, because He is in control, He is sovereign.

It is interesting to note that at one time, Christians applied this same thought process to evangelism. They believed that if God wanted people saved, He would do it with or without the help of missionaries and evangelists. Most Christians to-day reject this reasoning and see both the need for and the value in missionary work and evangelism. Unfortunately, many are still applying this kind of thinking to healing.

Taking such a radical position concerning God's sovereignty and His will sounds reasonable, but it is actually inconsistent with the Bible. For example, the Bible clearly teaches that it is God's will for all humans to be saved (Matthew 18:14; 2 Pet. 3:9; I Timothy 2:4). At the same time, there are many people in the world who are not saved. It would contradict Scripture, though, for us to conclude that this is God's will. There are other factors involved besides the will of God that affect whether or not a person is saved. So, just because there are sick people in the world, we should not and cannot assume that this is God's will.

One of the most powerful teachings that I can remember from my early days at the Vineyard was the concept of "the now and the not yet." John Wimber taught us that we live between the first and second comings of Christ. At His first coming, Jesus inaugurated the kingdom of God (Matthew 4:17; 12:28), but it is not yet present in its fullest expression (Matthew 25:31—33, 46). Wimber wrote:

> *"His sovereignty, lordship and kingdom are what brings healing. Our part is to pray 'Thy kingdom come" and trust him for whatever healing comes from His gracious hand. And if in this age it does not come, then we still have assurance from the atonement that it will come in the age to come."*

> - John Wimber

We know from the Scriptures that some things are a mystery to us (Deuteronomy 9:9), but as Christians we know that God is also willing to intervene in our lives as we engage Him through faith-filled prayer (Genesis 18:16—33; John 14:12—14). To better understand God's will towards healing, the best place to look is at the life and ministry of Jesus. He perfectly personified the heart and will of the Father. He was the visible image of the invisible God (Colossians 1:15).

> *"He is the image of the invisible God, the firstborn over all creation."*

According to Jesus, He did only what the Father wanted Him to do:

> *"Then Jesus answered and said to them, Most assuredly, I say to you, the Son can do nothing of Himself, but what He sees the Father do; for whatever He does, the Son also does in like manner."*

> - John 5:19

"And He who sent Me is with Me. The Father has not left Me alone, for I always do those things that please Him."

- John 8:29

"If I do not do the works of My Father, do not believe Me; but if I do, though you do not believe Me, believe the works, that you may know and believe that the Father is in Me, and I in Him"

- John 10:37-38

"Then Jesus cried out and said, He who believes in Me, believes not in Me but in Him who sent Me. And he who sees Me sees Him who sent Me."

- John 12:44-45

"Jesus said to him, Have I been with you so long, and yet you have not known Me, Philip? He who has seen Me has seen the Father; so how can you say, Show us the Father? Do you not believe that I am in the Father, and the Father in Me? The words that I speak to you I do not speak on My own authority; but the Father who dwells in Me does the works. Believe Me that I am in the Father and the Father in Me, or else believe Me for the sake of the works themselves."

- John 14:9-11

Clearly, these Scriptures demonstrate what God wants regarding healing by what Jesus did. In the gospel accounts, Jesus healed a lot! In fact, He healed every person who came to Him for healing. He even healed some who never asked for healing but were brought to Him for help by others.

Let's look at one of the many healing stories that are found in the gospels and use Jesus as our model for what God really wants.

"When He had come down from the mountain, great multitudes followed Him. And behold, a leper came and worshiped Him, saying, Lord, if You are willing, You can make me clean. Then Jesus put out His hand and touched him, saying, I am willing; be cleansed. Immediately his leprosy was cleansed. And Jesus said to him, See that you tell no one; but go your way, show yourself to the priest, and offer the gift that Moses commanded, as a testimony to them."

- Matthew 8:1-4

In Leviticus 13 and 14 we read about the laws relating to "leprosy" or what we would call Hansen's disease. Leprosy is highly infectious, being transmitted from person to person with incubation periods as short as just a few weeks. Left untreated, leprosy can be progressive, causing permanent damage to the skin, nerves, limbs and eyes. Secondary infections can result in tissue loss causing fingers and toes to become shortened and deformed, as cartilage is absorbed into the body. The Levitical laws governing this disease are recorded in verses 13:45-46.

"Now the leper on whom the sore is, his clothes shall be torn and his head bare; and he shall cover his mustache, and cry, Unclean! Unclean! He shall be unclean. All the days he has the sore he shall be unclean. He is unclean,

and he shall dwell alone; his dwelling shall be
outside the camp."

Skin ailments were probably common then in Israel, since Jesus mentions them in Matthew 10, when He sent out the twelve with authority to heal.

Like HIV today, there was tremendous social isolation and shame associated with leprosy. There was also the stigma that leprosy might be a curse sent from God (Numbers 12:10—12, Miriam afflicted with leprosy by God as judgment for her sin; Job 18:13).

In the Old Testament, healing from leprosy was rare and considered extremely difficult (2 Kings 5:7). Possibly this man and others believed God has deliberately cursed him with leprosy because of some sin he had committed.

Surprisingly, the man seemed to believe that Jesus could heal him. It wasn't that his disease was too difficult to heal or that Jesus lacked the power and ability. The real question for him was whether or not Jesus wanted to. It is clear that he wanted to be healed because he came out of the crowd and went right up to Jesus. Lepers were supposed to keep their distance from people, which the ten lepers in Luke 17:12—13 did. But this fellow came up close enough for Jesus to be able to reach out and touch him. He knew what he wanted; he just didn't know what Jesus had in mind. He believed in Jesus' power to heal, but was not sure about Jesus' desire to heal. Nowhere else in all the gospels did anyone ever ask Jesus if He was willing to heal!

This man's dilemma is very similar to ones today when Christians pray for healing. Believers often pray, "Lord, if it's your will, please heal Joe's back problem." Most likely this comes from an attempt to imitate Jesus' prayer in the Garden in Gethsemane, "Father, if it is Your will, take this cup away from Me; nevertheless not My will, but Yours, be done"

(Luke 22:42). However, it also reveals that we doubt God's willingness to heal. Many Christians assert that God can do anything, and that nothing is too difficult for Him, including the healing of a particular illness. It's His intentions that they are unsure of. How does God feel about the sickness? Does He care? Does He want to teach a lesson through the sickness? Will He teach and then alleviate it? What is God's will?

How did Jesus Heal?

Jesus healed this man differently than He did the ten lepers in Luke 17.

> *"Then as He entered a certain village, there met Him ten men who were lepers, who stood afar off. And they lifted up their voices and said, Jesus, Master, have mercy on us! So when He saw them, He said to them, Go, show yourselves to the priests. And so it was that as they went, they were cleansed."*

> - Luke 17:12-14

In that instance, He simply spoke to them (Luke 17:14). But with this man, Jesus first reached out and touched him. The law forbade such an action since lepers were unclean and anyone touching them would become unclean as well. Jesus disregarded the regulations and touched the man first, to demonstrate His willingness to heal. He also told the man that He was willing, so that by word and deed, the man would be convinced of Jesus' desire to heal. He then spoke a command that resulted in the man's healing from the leprosy. A touch from Jesus made the man clean, rather than the leper making Jesus unclean! Nothing Jesus touches can remain defiled.

Note that Jesus did not rebuke or correct the man for asking Him if He was willing to heal. Jesus seemed only too happy to prove that He was willing. In contrast, Jesus corrected the father of the demonized boy in Mark 9:21—27 for questioning His ability to heal:

> *"So He asked his father, How long has this been happening to him? And he said, 'From childhood. And often he has thrown him both into the fire and into the water to destroy him. But if You can do anything, have compassion on us and help us.' Jesus said to him, 'If you can believe, all things are possible to him who believes.' Immediately the father of the child cried out and said with tears, 'Lord, I believe; help my unbelief!' When Jesus saw that the people came running together, He rebuked the unclean spirit, saying to it, Deaf and dumb spirit, I command you, come out of him and enter him no more! Then the spirit cried out, convulsed him greatly, and came out of him. And he became as one dead, so that many said, 'He is dead.' But Jesus took him by the hand and lifted him up, and he arose"*

For Jesus, to question or doubt God's ability and power was ridiculous!

> *"So Jesus said to them, Because of your unbelief; for assuredly, I say to you, if you have faith as a mustard seed, you will say to this mountain, Move from here to there, and it will move; and nothing will be impossible for you. However, this kind does not go out except by prayer and fasting."*

> - Matthew 17:20-21

Jesus forcefully confronted unbelief wherever He found it. However, He seemed to deal more gently with doubt in His willingness to heal (Matthew 12:20).

> *"A bruised reed He will not break,*
>
> *And smoking flax He will not quench,*
>
> *Till He sends forth justice to victory..."*

Jesus told the man to go show himself to the priest so that he may be declared "clean," in accordance with the law in Leviticus 14. Because this disease had social ramifications, the healing needed to be confirmed in a social situation. For the man to be completely healed, he had to be recognized as "clean" by the priests so that he could re-enter society and resume living as a healed person.

Some people actively engaged in the healing ministry discourage the use of medicine and medical professionals. Yet, we see that Jesus instructed this man to follow the conventional course of his day and go to the priests to be declared healed by them. It wasn't that Jesus' word was inadequate. Confirmation from others can help solidify the miracle for the person who was healed. It's also clear that Jesus' motivation was not to further publicize Himself since He told the man to tell no one else about what had happened.

Compassion and Mercy

> *"Then Jesus, moved with compassion, stretched out His hand and touched him, and said to him, I am willing; be cleansed."*

> - Mark 1:41

The compassion of Jesus is explicitly mentioned in several healing accounts in the Gospels and perhaps assumed in most.

> *"And when Jesus went out He saw a great multitude; and He was moved with compassion for them, and healed their sick"*

> *- Mark 14:14*

Compassion and mercy is key to understanding God's will or desire to heal. We know it is possible for a person to be able but unwilling to help in a situation because of stinginess, indifference, or just plain selfishness. The attitude of the heart is key to the will. The God of the universe is able to do anything He wants. But He has a choice. It is God's attitude—how he feels towards the sick—that determines His willingness to heal. When we look at Jesus, we find a person who was always willing to heal the sick. This should tell us volumes about God's will concerning healing.

Jesus is our model

Dr. Ken Blue, author, consultant, and conference speaker, pointed out the challenge of many healing models today.

> *"In reading the New Testament, I was initially disturbed to see that Jesus healed the sick and cast out demons very differently from the way we do it today. Every healing ministry I am familiar with depends largely on prayer. Jesus healed primarily by command. Unlike His followers today, he did not petition for healing; he pronounced it."*

Jesus commissioned the twelve and later seventy-two other disciples to go from town to town, preaching the kingdom and healing the sick:

> *"Then He called His twelve disciples together and gave them power and authority over all demons, and to cure diseases. He sent them to preach the kingdom of God and to heal the sick."*
>
> - Luke 9:1-2

> *"After these things the Lord appointed seventy others also, and sent them two by two before His face into every city and place where He Himself was about to go. Then He said to them, The harvest truly is great, but the laborers are few; therefore pray the Lord of the harvest to send out laborers into His harvest ... And heal the sick there, and say to them, The kingdom of God has come near to you"*
>
> - Luke 10:1-2; 9

In other words, He commissioned His followers to do His ministry. In Acts 1:1, Luke implied that the apostles were continuing to do what Jesus began in His earthly ministry.

> *"The former account I made, O Theophilus, of all that Jesus began both to do and teach..."*
>
> - Acts 1:1

Second, in John 14, Jesus tells His disciples that if they believe in Him, they will do what He had been doing! In fact, Jesus tells them that whatever they ask He will do it.

*"Most assuredly, I say to you, he who believes in Me,
the works that I do he will do also; and greater
works than these he will do, because I go to My Father. And whatever you ask in My name, that I will
do, that the Father may be glorified in the Son. If you
ask anything in My name, I will do it"*

- John 14:12-14

What had Jesus been doing? He ministered by preaching and
teaching about the kingdom of God and healing the sick:

*"And Jesus went about all Galilee, teaching in their
synagogues, preaching the gospel of the kingdom,
and healing all kinds of sickness and all kinds of disease among the people"*

- Matthew 4:23

*"When evening had come, they brought to Him
many who were demon- possessed. And He cast out
the spirits with a word, and healed all who were
sick, Peter's Mother- in- Law Healed that it might be
fulfilled which was spoken by Isaiah the prophet,
saying: He Himself took our infirmities and bore our
sicknesses."*

- Matthew 8:16-17

*"Then Jesus went about all the cities and villages,
teaching in their synagogues, preaching the gospel
of the kingdom, and healing every sickness and every disease among the people"*

- Matthew 9:35

*"Jesus answered and said to them, Go and tell John
the things which you hear and see: The blind see
and the lame walk; the lepers are cleansed and the
deaf hear; the dead are raised up and the poor have
the gospel preached to them."*

- Matthew 11:4-5

*"And when Jesus went out He saw a great multitude;
and He was moved with compassion for them, and
healed their sick."*

- Matthew 14:14

*"At evening, when the sun had set, they brought to
Him all who were sick and those who were demon.
And the whole city was gathered together at the
door. Then He healed many who were sick with various diseases, and cast out many demons; and He
did not allow the demons to speak, because they
knew Him."*

- Mark 1:32-34

*"When the sun was setting, all those who had any
that were sick with various diseases brought them
to Him; and He laid His hands on every one of them
and healed them. And demons also came out of
many, crying out and saying, You are the Christ, the
Son of God."*

- Luke 4:40-41

*"And He came down with them and stood on a level
place with a crowd of His disciples and a great multitude of people from all Judea and Jerusalem, and
from the seacoast of Tyre and Sidon, who came to*

hear Him and be healed of their diseases, as well as those who were tormented with unclean spirits. And they were healed. And the whole multitude sought to touch Him, for power went out from Him and healed them all."

- Luke 6:17-19

"But when the multitudes knew it, they followed Him; and He received them and spoke to them about the kingdom of God, and healed those who had need of healing."

- Luke 9:11

"Then a great multitude followed Him, because they saw His signs which He performed on those who were diseased."

- John 6:2

We must remember that the biblical notion of a disciple was not someone who followed just the teachings of Jesus or only intellectually assented to His message. A disciple, according to the New Testament, was someone who followed Jesus in every way, doing the same things He did. Therefore a disciple imitated His teacher. In order for us to imitate our Lord, let's examine the ministry of Jesus more closely and discover what some essential ingredients are for healing the sick.

Authority and Power

Compare the words "authority" in Matthew 10:1 with "power" in Luke 5:17.

> *"And when He had called His twelve disciples to Him, He gave them power (Greek: exousia meaning authority) over unclean spirits, to cast them out, and to heal all kinds of sickness and all kinds of disease."*
>
> - John 6:2

> *"Now it happened on a certain day, as He was teaching, that there were Pharisees and teachers of the law sitting by, who had come out of every town of Galilee, Judea, and Jerusalem. And the power (Greek: dynamis meaning power) of the Lord was present to heal them."*
>
> - Luke 5:17

Are they the same thing? How do they each play a role in the way God heals the sick?

While there is some overlap between authority and power, there is an important difference, especially as we consider healing. Authority to heal means the right to heal. Jesus had the right to order sickness to leave a person's body. The sickness had to obey Jesus' authority. Power to heal implies the ability to heal. In Luke 5:17, Luke wrote, "the power of the Lord was present for him to heal the sick." It seems there were special times and situations when the power to heal the sick was with Jesus (which would imply that there were other times when it was not with Him). Jesus conveyed this when He said that He was not able to do anything apart from the Father (John 5:19).

> *"Then Jesus answered and said to them, Most assuredly, I say to you, the Son can do nothing of Himself, but what He sees the Father do; for whatever He does, the Son also does in like manner."*

The key for Jesus seemed to be the will of the Father, "what the Father was doing."

In the Greek, this difference is even clearer. The Greek word for "power" in Luke 5:17 is "*dynamis*," from where we get our English word "dynamite." It means "power, strength, ability or might." This kind of power is inherent power, power residing in a thing by virtue of its nature, or for example, when a person exerts or puts forth effort. The Greek word for "authority" in Matthew 10:1 is "*exousia*." It means "authority, right or jurisdiction." This kind of authority is the right of influence, the right to rule and govern, or the right to have one's commands submitted to an obeyed by others.

A traffic officer can illustrate the difference between "power" and "authority" in the way we are using them. A policeman or policewoman who is directing traffic does not stop cars by his or her own physical power and might, but by the authority that has been given to him or her by the state. He or she holds up a hand, and the traffic must obey or suffer the consequences. It is absurd to imagine an officer physically stopping each car with just bare hands! In contrast, the general public cannot stop traffic with a raised hand because we do not have the same authority.

This does not mean that authority is all we need in healing. According to the New Testament, Jesus had both the authority and the power to heal the sick.

At the end of Matthew's gospel, Jesus declares that all authority on heaven and in earth have been given to Him (28:18).

> *"And Jesus came and spoke to them, saying, All authority has been given to Me in heaven and on earth."*

Jesus then commands His disciples to reproduce themselves by making disciples of all nations. Along with sharing the gospel and baptizing new converts, His followers were to teach succeeding generations to obey everything He had commanded them (28:19—20).

> *"Go therefore and make disciples of all the nations, baptizing them in the name of the Father and of the Son and of the Holy Spirit, teaching them to observe all things that I have commanded you; and lo, I am with you always, even to the end of the age. Amen."*

That "everything" included Jesus' delegating the authority and power to heal, cast out demons, etc.

He uses us...

So, the way that God heals the sick is by using us. He delegates the authority [right] and the ability [power] to heal to His followers. This may be a very different concept from what we have always believed about healing. Many of us picture God doing all the healing directly from heaven as we petition Him. But according to the New Testament, God has given that responsibility to us. He heals the sick through us, His church. It is worth noting that nowhere does Jesus tell His disciples to merely pray for the sick and hope for the best. He tells them to heal the sick!

In Luke 9:1, Jesus gave the disciples both the power and the authority to drive out demons and to cure diseases. When we pray for the sick, there is often a lot of God's power present, and the person receiving prayer and those praying can feel it. But we must keep in mind that we do not possess or own the power to heal. We have been delegated the authority to heal, and when we move in that authority and pray for a sick person, then God sends His power to accomplish the healing.

> *"Then He called His twelve disciples together and gave them power and authority over all demons, and to cure diseases. He sent them to preach the kingdom of God and to heal the sick."*

> *- Luke 9:1-2*

A brief study of the gospels reveals at least ten was that Jesus healed the sick:

- Jesus healed by the Word (Mark 3:1-6, Psalm 107:20)
- Jesus healed by Faith (Luke 7:1-10, Romans 10:8)
- Jesus healed to release those bound by the demonic (Mark 1:23-27)
- Jesus healed to restore life (Mark 1:40-45)

- Jesus healed through the faith of others (Mark 2:1-12)
- Jesus healed through deliverance (Matthew 12:22-37, Matthew 17:14-21, Luke 13:10-17, Mark 5:1-20, Acts 10:38)
- Jesus healed the desperate (Mark 5:25-34, 41)
- Jesus healed the persistent (Matthew 15:22-28)
- Jesus healed to reveal the heart of the Father (John 9:5-34)
- Jesus healed His enemies (Luke 22:49-51

Isaiah saw the nature and power of the atonement in regards to healing when he recorded in Isaiah 53:

> *"Who has believed our report? And to whom has the arm of the Lord been revealed? For He shall grow up before Him as a tender plant, and as a root out of dry ground. He has no form or comeliness; and when we see Him, there is no beauty that we should desire Him. He is despised and rejected by men, a Man of sorrows and acquainted with grief. And we hid, as it were, our faces from Him; He was despised, and we did not esteem Him.*
>
> *Surely He has borne our griefs and carried our sorrows; Yet we esteemed Him stricken, smitten by God, and afflicted. But He was wounded for our transgressions, He was bruised for our iniquities; The chastisement for our peace was upon Him, and by His stripes we are healed."*

- Isaiah 53:1-5

Matthew confirms this attribute of salvation when he writes:

"Now when Jesus had come into Peter's house, He saw his wife's mother lying sick with a fever. So He touched her hand, and the fever left her. And she arose and served them. When evening had come, they brought to Him many who were demon-possessed. And He cast out the spirits with a word, and healed all who were sick, that it might be fulfilled which was spoken by Isaiah the prophet, saying: He Himself took our infirmities and bore our sicknesses."

- Matthew 8:14-18

As does Peter:

"...who Himself bore our sins in His own body on the tree, that we, having died to sins, might live for righteousness—by whose stripes you were healed."

- 1 Peter 2:24

The scriptures also outline at least eleven ways in which the body of Christ operates in the healing ministry.

- The anointing and presence of the gift of healing (Acts 19:11-12; 1 Corinthians 12:9).
- The laying on of hands (Mark 16:8).
- Elders, prayer, and anointing oil (James 5:14).
- Speaking the Word to sickness (Mark 11:23; Psalms 107:20).
- The power of agreement (Matthew 18:19-20; Psalms 133).
- Your own faith (Mark 11:24).
- The name of Jesus (John 14:13-14; Acts 3:1-8).
- Praying for others (Job 42:10).

- The faith of others (Mark 2:5-11).
- Healing through Communion (1 Corinthians 11:22-26; 1 John 1:7; Isaiah 52:5; 1 Peter 2:24; Isaiah 52:14; 1 Corinthians 11:29-30).
- Medicine and the medical profession.

Healing comes in many forms. A simple walk through the book of Acts and we see several dimensions. I love the book of Acts because it reveals the church in action!

- To be strengthened (Acts 3:7)
- To be healed (Acts 3:11)
- To be whole (Acts 3:16)
- To be saved - sozo (Acts 4:9)
- To be cleansed (Acts 4:10)
- To be given therapy (Acts 4:14)

The more we study the New Testament, the more we should be convinced that healing the sick is something God wants us, His church, to do today. As we obey the Lord by praying for the sick, we realize that we cannot operate on our own. We need to recognize the chain of command from the Father, to the Lord Jesus, to us.

We live in a day of incredible urgency. The world looks for a sign that God is with them and for them. You are that sign. Step out and let the healing begin!

We are privileged to have His authority to heal the sick, but we must remain in relationship with Him and focus on His will being done. He has been given the right to govern all the affairs of heaven and earth. We need to obey Him, by the power of His Spirit within us. We need to live as foot soldiers under the command of our King, and like the centurion, say that we are people under authority who have been given authority...to heal. Thankfully, we have His promise to be with us always as we follow in His footsteps.

CHAPTER 3

Healing and Seeing

*"Then your light shall break forth like the
morning, your healing shall spring forth speedily,
and your righteousness shall go before you; the
glory of the Lord shall be your rear guard"*

– Isaiah 58:8

Healing and prophetic ministry have been linked together many times throughout the Scriptures. Often times, this happened through prophetic declaration, action, or the command to do something and if you do it you shall be healed.

The story of Elijah and the widow's son is a perfect example of a prophetic action comingled with compassion, relationship, and healing.

> *"Now it happened after these things that the
> son of the woman who owned the house be-
> came sick. And his sickness was so serious that
> there was no breath left in him.*
>
> *So she said to Elijah, What have I to do with
> you, O man of God? Have you come to me to*

> *bring my sin to remembrance, and to kill my son?*
>
> *And he said to her, Give me your son. So he took him out of her arms and carried him to the upper room where he was staying, and laid him on his own bed.*
>
> *Then he cried out to the Lord and said, O Lord my God, have You also brought tragedy on the widow with whom I lodge, by killing her son? And he stretched himself out on the child three times, and cried out to the Lord and said, O Lord my God, I pray, let this child's soul come back to him.*
>
> *Then the Lord heard the voice of Elijah; and the soul of the child came back to him, and he revived"*
>
> *- 1 Kings 17:17-24*

In this example we see Elijah responding to the widow's request to heal her son, but literally raise him from the dead. In anguish, he carried the child to the upper room where he was staying. Placed him on his bed and laid on him. While he lay on his breathless body he cried out to the Lord in a deep prayer. At the moment Elijah HEARD the voice of the Lord, the child came back to life. This is a very powerful example of how the "hearing ear" is critical to the ministry of healing, what God is saying regarding the illness.

Another good example of this is found in the book of Numbers. In this book, we find three instances where Moses intercedes for the healing of his people. The first instance is that of Miriam's leprosy:

"Then Miriam and Aaron spoke against Moses because of the Ethiopian woman whom he had married; for he had married an Ethiopian woman. So they said, "Has the Lord indeed spoken only through Moses? Has He not spoken through us also?" And the Lord heard it. (Now the man Moses was very humble, more than all men who were on the face of the earth.)

Suddenly, the Lord said to Moses, Aaron, and Miriam, "Come out, you three, to the tabernacle of meeting!" So the three came out. Then the Lord came down in the pillar of cloud and stood in the door of the tabernacle, and called Aaron and Miriam. And they both went forward.

Then He said, "Hear now My words: If there is a prophet among you, I, the Lord, make Myself known to him in a vision; I speak to him in a dream. Not so with My servant Moses; He is faithful in all My house. I speak with him face to face, Even plainly, and not in dark sayings; And he sees the form of the Lord. Why then were you not afraid to speak against My servant Moses?

So the anger of the Lord was aroused against them, and He departed. And when the cloud departed from above the tabernacle, Suddenly, Miriam became leprous, as white as snow. Then Aaron turned toward Miriam, and there she was, a leper. So Aaron said to Moses, "Oh, my lord! Please do not lay this sin on us, in which we have done foolishly and in which we have sinned. Please do not let her be as one dead, whose flesh is half consumed when he comes out of his mother's womb!

So Moses cried out to the Lord, saying, "Please heal her, O God, I pray!"

Then the Lord said to Moses, "If her father had but spit in her face, would she not be shamed seven days? Let her be shut out of the camp seven days, and afterward she may be received again." So Miriam was shut out of the camp seven days, and the people did not journey till Miriam was brought in again."

- Numbers 12:1-15

In this story we see Miriam and Aaron speaking out against Moses regarding his marriage and their justification for doing so rested in the offices that they held. Miriam was a prophetess, and Aaron received revelation by the Urim and Thummim, yet their conclusion was wrong and the result was the judgment of God bringing about Miriam's Leprosy.

Then Moses cried unto the Lord and pleaded with God to heal her. God replied:

> *"Then the Lord said to Moses, "If her father had but spit in her face, would she not be shamed seven days? Let her be shut out of the camp seven days, and afterward she may be received again." (vs. 14)*

This is the command to do something. The implication is - if you put her out for seven days and let my judgment rest I will heal her, and in verse 15 we see obedience to this declaration of the Lord. Another interesting fact about this story is the prophet's ability to only know in part and see in part or see through a glass darkly, and in the case of this book, through visions and dreams. This comes out in the comparison between the ministry of Moses and that of the normal prophet.

Therefore it is critical for the seer to use wisdom's ways and let meekness usher forth as fruit from his spirit, lest he speak presumptuously, resulting in a false word, bringing about hurt to others. For unlike Moses we will only know in part and see in part until we stand face to face with Him who knows all things. Now let's look at Moses receiving a directive that calls for action. It is found in Numbers.

> "And the people spoke against God and against Moses: "Why have you brought us up out of Egypt to die in the wilderness? For there is no food and no water, and our soul loathes this worthless bread." So the Lord sent fiery serpents among the people, and they bit the people; and many of the people of Israel died.
>
> Therefore the people came to Moses, and said, "We have sinned, for we have spoken against the Lord and against you; pray to the Lord that He take away the serpents from us." So Moses prayed for the people.
>
> Then the Lord said to Moses, "Make a fiery serpent, and set it on a pole; and it shall be that everyone who is bitten, when he looks at it, shall live." So Moses made a bronze serpent, and put it on a pole; and so it was, if a serpent had bitten anyone, when he looked at the bronze serpent, he lived."

- Numbers 21:5-8

Again, we see here sickness because of the judgment of God. So Moses prays and intercedes for the people and the Lord's response to him is twofold, make thee a fiery serpent, - and for the people - who ever looks upon the serpent shall live. Here obedience is twofold. On the one hand, the prophet Moses has a task he must do, and on the other hand, the people have to respond to the Lord by looking upon that serpent of brass. Therefore, we see conditional healing based upon prophetic obedience and prophetic response. It is also interesting to note that, typologically, the serpent points to Christ on the cross taking the curse upon himself, for by His stripes we are healed. For even here, we see that the testimony of Jesus is the spirit of prophecy.

A study of the gospels reveals that this kind of "action," is also seen in the healing ministry of Jesus. We know that Jesus laid aside his divine nature and took the form of a servant relying completely upon the Holy Spirit for direction. Jesus himself stated, "*I only do what I see the Father doing.*" In the book of Mark, we read the story of a man born blind who had desired to touch Jesus that he may be healed. Jesus' response to this man is unusual.

> "*So He took the blind man by the hand and led him out of the town. And when He had spit on his eyes and put His hands on him, He asked him if he saw anything. And he looked up and said, "I see men like trees, walking." Then He put His hands on his eyes again and made him look up. And he was restored and saw everyone clearly.*"

> - Mark 8:23-25

We know that Jesus could have just spoken the word and the man would have been healed but he did not. I believe the reason for this is a response to the Father giving Him an "action" to perform, when completed, then and only then, would the man be made whole. The key here is relationship with God and obedience to all that he commands you to do. It takes a Rhema from heaven for a specific situation to get God's desired results.

We know what God's general will is, that by His stripes we are made whole. Yet, just the proclamation of that truth is not enough. You have to listen, listen, and listen again, keeping your eyes on Jesus for He has said, *"...As the Father has sent me so I send you."* Let's go therefore and follow His example for we are members of His body - but He is the head - the chief cornerstone.

We could also spend time talk of the many wonderful things the Lord has done through his prophets. We could speak of Elisha healing the waters, the healing of Jeroboam and the man of God, Isaiah and Hezekiah's health, but now let me share with you some personal experiences that will elaborate the subject of seeing and healing.

Illustrative Example

Say unto that Mountain, Flee...

In 1981 my wife Jan and I moved to a little town up in the mountains of Southern California. We had been married two years and I had been saved just over a year. As stated earlier, our hope was to find a Calvary Chapel, like Wimber's. We were very excited to find Calvary Chapel Conference Center in Twin Peaks, just outside Lake Arrowhead. Combined with the trees and the serenity of the mountains this was a perfect place to move into a deeper relationship with the Spirit of God.

We arrived at this mountain retreat, shortly after Lonnie Frisbee had been introduced, and a revival had broken out that changed the mountain and the atmosphere of church. It was truly electrifying. Our first summer there I started attending a home fellowship group. During this time, I experienced a presence of the Holy Spirit that I had never encountered before.

One night, while at a home group meeting, in the middle of worship, the Spirit of God came upon me in beautiful waves of grace. I was kneeling down praising God with my hands in the air when Suddenly, the presence of God was all over me. Like electricity over my entire body, I was raptured into His presence. Suddenly, the muscles in my body began to contort and my hands began to fold up in a spastic matter. My eyes started to flutter, my lips began to shake, and my speech was slurred and muffled. The effect was overwhelming - incredible joy mingled with incredible pain. All I could do was praise Him with contorted arms, hands, face, and lips. My speech had left me. I was completely disabled.

This experienced lasted for well over an hour. I didn't really know what was going on but I knew it was God and that the Lord was doing something. This experience happened to me every week during our season in this mountain resort. After about a year, we left Lake Arrowhead and moved to Palm Springs, a desert community south of Lake Arrowhead. We began attending Vineyard Christian Fellowship in Palm Desert. It would be five years later that God would reveal to me what He was doing. At that time it was only on occasion, about every three months or so, that I would feel this intense outpouring of deformity and praise but every time it happened I found myself raptured in intersession.

In the summer of 1986, I attended a conference at the Anaheim Vineyard - Healing 86 - with John Wimber and Francis & Judith MacNutt. During the second night of this conference, we were in the middle of worship when Suddenly, the Spirit of God was on me more powerful than I had ever experienced before. His presence was just like that season up in the mountains five years earlier only more intense and this time accompanied by visions and words from the throne of God.

I sat in my chair, arms bent, eyes fluttering, fingers, and hands curled in a prenatal position as the power of God moved through my body. The deformity was overwhelming. With slurred speech, all I could do was praise Him. Suddenly, in the midst of this awkward trance-like outpouring, I heard the voice of God,

> *"Say to that mountain - Flee into the sea. Say to that mountain FLEE into the sea - SAY TO THAT MOUNTAIN - FLEE INTO THE SEA!"*

Then I saw the Word of God, larger than life, open against the black of night - then the wind began to blow - moving briskly upon the pages of the Bible and the words came alive as the pages began to flutter, turning, as if the fingers of the Spirit hovered above the Word of God.

I heard the Lord speak again,

> *"SAY UNTO THAT MOUNTAIN - FLEE INTO THE SEA. - For surely as My word stands and My wind blows, I, the Lord, shall cause it to come about. With every turning of the page so she shall be made whole and as each page quivers before My presence surely I will free this child in bondage. So SAY TO THAT MOUNTAIN FLEE INTO THE SEA!"*

Then I saw a mountain, tall and intimidating, beginning to crumble and I looked and the mountain was gone and in its place I saw a mother sitting on the floor with a child's head resting in her lap. The child's body was bent and twisted and the mother was wiping drool from the corner of her mouth. She appeared to be crippled by an extreme case of Muscular Dystrophy or Multiple Sclerosis. It was then that I realized the pain in my body *was her pain* and the bentness I was ex-periencing *was her bentness...* and tears began to roll down the sides of my face. After that, I saw the same picture of the Word of God as before, with the pages slowly moving one after the other, only this time as each page turned the pain in my body began to disappear and the spasmodic deformity of my muscles slowly began to relax.

Finely the event was over and my speech slowly began to return. When I came to, the worship was over and John Wimber had finished his lecture and was calling for a brief break in the service. I knew with all my heart that this moth-er with her withered child was at this conference and that

God wanted me to find them and share with them my experience. I grabbed my Bible and began walking through the aisles of this crowed auditorium of 5,000 people, looking for this family I saw in the vision.

As I turned down the first aisle, I looked towards the back of the auditorium, in my amazement, I saw on the floor in the back a woman stroking the hair of a young girl and whipping spittle away from her mouth. It was then that I felt the presence of the Lord and I knew that this was the woman in my vision.

With hesitation, I walked up to them and sat beside the mother. All of a sudden, I realized that what I had to say was a prophetic word calling for prophetic action on the part of the mother. She had come to this conference wanting her daughter to be healed and God sent her a message of faith and action pointing to the gradual healing of this lovely young girl. She was to stand firm and the word made Rhema – would move her into a prayer position of saying to that mountain - **FLEE INTO THE SEA.**

We sat together, prayed, talked, and praised the Lord our God. I had reached out for this young daughter's twisted arm and asked the Lord of life to bring the reality of His Word to this young lady. Suddenly, this girl's hand began to move in a way that it never moved before. I looked at the mother and tears began to flow down her checks - she knew what God had spoken will surly come to pass. After an hour, I left this couple and headed back to my seat.

When I got back to my hotel room that night the Lord spoke to me and said,

"You will see her tomorrow - ask her, when did this first happen to your daughter?"

I responded, "Yes Lord."

That night I lay on my bed, blown away by the night's events. In the morning, I rushed to the back of the auditorium eagerly searching for the woman and her child but could not find them. In frustration, I thought to myself - how am I going to find them among all these people. I went to get a cup of coffee. As I headed for my seat, I bumped into someone, when I turned around to apologize; I was staring into that mother's eyes.

She was so excited, jumping up and down saying, "Praise God, Praise God, - thank you for that word last night, last night she moved in a way she never moved before - and I know every move of my little girl."

"Praise God," I said not believing my eyes. I looked at her glowing countenance and asked her when her daughter became ill.

She responded, "She's been like this for five years."

Then my eyes began to tear up, the presence of God was all over me. I began to explain to her what happened to me up on the mountain five years earlier. I realized that *the very moment* this girl was struck-down with this devastating illness, the Lord felt her pain, heard her cries, and **took the pain into Himself.** Then, in a way I don't understand, He distributed that pain through His body, the church, and prophetically caused a member of the body of Christ (me) to bear the burden for this wounded child, up on that mountain, **until the day we would meet and God would command that mountain to flee into the sea.**

The flesh can't create this reaction only the Spirit can truly manifest this kind of intense intercession with manifestations of bearing the burdens of others. The Spirit of God intercedes on behalf of the afflicted causing us to partner with Him - like Jesus in the garden of Gethsemane ushering forth tears of blood on the way to the cross. Therefore, in like manner, we come to the garden before we go to the cross so that the blood shed in the garden can be mingled with that precious blood spilt at the cross of the Lord. That action brings about the power of God to the one we bleed for in prayer.

Her response was overwhelming for at that moment, with all the doubts of the past and wondering if God had ever heard her prayers, she was ushered to the omnipotence of ALL MIGHTY GOD. She knew that He who sits on the throne is all-powerful and that He has always been with them working out the answer to her cries.

This experience for me was truly life changing. When I read in the Scriptures about Hosea's entire life being a prophetic word to the nation of Israel I am blown away by the depth of His involvement. When I look at the unusual acts of Jeremiah and Ezekiel, the depth of the actions the Lord uses in dealing with the nation intrigues me. When I read Isaiah 53:4-5 and hear him, speak of the ministry of the Messiah:

> *"Surely He has borne our griefs, and carried our sorrows; Yet we esteemed Him stricken,*

*Smitten by God, and afflicted. But He was wounded for our transgressions, He was bruised for our iniquities; The chastisement for our peace was upon Him, **and by His stripes we are healed.***"

I know He has made a way for the afflicted. I understand His heart to those in dire need and the depth of His Love blows me away. The seer application is evident, Jesus Christ distributed the pain of this child to His body, the church; He released the spirit of intercession and burden bearing for a space of five years. It was only at that perfect moment in time that He opened the windows of Heaven and revealed His complete plan and purpose for this child. The answer came through a vision during a moment of bliss in His presence. However, the real work, I believe happened during that five-year period where the Holy Spirit cradled this child to the point of breakthrough.

CHAPTER 4

Directional Seeing

"Arise and go to the street called Straight, and inquire at the house of Judas for one called Saul of Tarsus, for behold, he is praying. And in a vision he has seen a man named Ananias coming in and putting his hand on him, so that he might receive his sight."

- Acts 9:11-12

Seeing What to Do

"And he was three days without sight, and neither ate nor drank. Now there was a certain disciple at Damascus named Ananias; and to him the Lord said in a vision, "Ananias."

And he said, "Here I am, Lord."

So the Lord said to him, "Arise and go to the street called Straight, and inquire at the house of Judas for one called Saul of Tarsus, for behold, he is praying. And in a vision he has seen a man named Ananias coming in and putting his hand on him, so that he might receive his sight."

Then Ananias answered, "Lord, I have heard from many about this man, how much harm he has done to Your saints in Jerusalem. And here he has authority from the chief priests to bind all who call on Your name."

But the Lord said to him, "Go, for he is a chosen vessel of Mine to bear My name before Gentiles, kings, and the children of Israel. For I will show him how many things he must suffer for My name's sake."

And Ananias went his way and entered the house; and laying his hands on him he said, "Brother Saul, the Lord Jesus, who appeared to you on the road as you came, has sent me that you may receive your sight and be filled with the Holy Spirit." Immediately there fell from his eyes something like scales, and he received his sight at once; and he arose and was baptized." - Act 9:10-18

Often times the Lord will use visions or dreams to communicate who he wants to heal and what he wants you to do in reference to this healing. **Remember a condition revealed is a condition to be healed.** This kind of vision applies not only to healing but also to ministerial direction in general. A perfect example of this is found in the book of Acts.

This story like no other in scripture touches my heart the deepest. It brings me back to that Christmas Eve where Jesus confronted me on my own road to Damascus and several weeks later where He entered into my heart, removed the scales from my eyes, and brought me into the kingdom of God. Oh how consistent is the Lord our God - Oh how majestic is His name among those who fear Him.

In this story, we see Saul confronted by the Lord Jesus Christ on his way to persecute the church and due to this Glorious encounter, he is struck blind for a period of three days. After this period of what I suppose was a time of urgent prayer and repentance Saul pours out his heart to the one he meets along the way and is struck with a vision of a man named Ananias laying hands on him that he may receive his sight.

Now, in blindness, he waits for this promise of healing to be fulfilled. He wrestles with the issues of Judgment and Grace. He must have thought this blindness was a fitting punishment for one who lashed out at the Lord with religiously blind eyes. I suppose he never thought of seeing again. Yet for the first time in his life he is about to experience the grace of the cross and for this man of the law it would become the central themes throughout his ministry.

On the other side of this story, we have Ananias. Little is known about this man. We know that he was a disciple living in Damascus. He must have known that this persecutor of the saints was on his way there to destroy the church. Paul tells us later that Ananias was a devout observer of the law and highly respected by all the Jews living.

I find it very fitting to see how the Lord had chosen this potential martyr to be the one who would minister the grace of God to Saul. Ananias was a man who at one time had like passions as Saul but now was a disciple of Christ. In spite of his fear, the Lord chose him to minister to Saul, an enemy of the church. It is also interesting that Ananias is the Greek form of the Hebrew word "Hananyah" meaning "Jehovah has been gracious." You almost see prophetic play on words in this act of ministry to Saul.

Now let's look at the vision itself. It appears that this vision is something very natural. Ananias is not surprised that God is communicating to him in a vision. I am sure Peter's words on the day of Pentecost are fresh within his mind and that the church is the fulfillment of the words of the Prophet Joel. On the contrary he dialogues with the Lord, talking one on one if you will, trying to gain greater understanding on of this commission, and sharing with the Lord his personal fears. In like manner, the Lord responds to his concerns and tells him why he must minister to this man.

So here, we see visions, as a medium of communication to both the one administering healing as well as the recipient of the healing gift.

First, a vision is used by the Lord to communicate to the one being commissioned or sent out to heal, minister, or be the agent in healing.

- He received information as to the nature of the illness.
- He received information as to the identity of the person needing ministry.
- He received direction and the action to be taken when ministering the healing.

Second, vision is used by the Lord to communicate to the person in need of healing, the one on the receiving end of God's grace.

- Which brought about the promise of healing.
- He was shown how the healing will come about.
- He was shown who will be God's instrument in bringing about this healing.

All of which bring about the power of faith in the omnipotent Lord of glory.

Illustrative Examples

Cradle in the wind

Let me share with you another story from my own experience to elaborate on healing and directional seeing. Several years ago while working for Dr. Pat Robertson at the Christian Broadcasting Network in Virginia Beach, Virginia, I had a vision involving my administrative assistant, Janice.

Janice is a sweet spirited young lady who had been suffering with problems in her upper back and legs, which was a kind of scoliosis of the spine. This condition had brought her serious pain. We had prayed for her healing on several occasions but no results. Then, to my surprise, there were conditions of inner healing that the Lord had prioritized over the physical healing of her body.

One night while sleeping, I had a dream. In this dream, I was walking through the employee cafeteria at the Founders Inn and saw Janice sitting at a table eating lunch. The Lord spoke and said, "Go and pray for her that I may heal her." Then I saw myself walking towards Janice. I laid my hand on her shoulder and immediately she stood and began twisting and turning her back. As she was twisting and turning, to my amazement, she was transformed into a young girl. Then I heard the Lord say,

"I want to heal the child within."

After that, I saw a country road and at the end of the road was a white country church with double doors in the front of it. I walked up, opened the door, and saw Janice siting at an organ playing praises to the Lord. Janice's face was glowing, she had a crown on her head, and on her fingers were rings full of colorful jewels. The Lord spoke to me and said,

"Janice's entire life is music to my ears. She has blessed Me with the melody of her heart therefore I have crowned her with the sweetness of My Spirit - that she may play her song to the rest of My Bride. I have placed My rings upon her fingers that she may reach out to others and share what is truly music to my ears."

Then I woke, and the Lord said,

"Fred tell her."

I was so excited for her, and blown away by the Lord's incredible passionate heart. I rushed to work and found Janise busily working in the office. I shared with her the dream that the Lord had given me and asked her if I could pray for her. With tears running down her face, she bowed her head and we began to pray. In the midst of praying, the Lord gave me a vision.

In this vision, I saw a tree - it was an autumn tree with amber leaves. One of the leaves on this tree started to fall to the ground and I saw the wind rise up, and like a baby's cradle, gently enfolded the leaf and bring it to the ground.

As I shared this picture with Janice, the Lord told me to tell her the following:

> *"Janice, do not be afraid. My love for you passes all understanding, and your life is truly music to my ears. You are in a season of change. I have come to bring life to that child within you... to that little girl that thinks she's not loved... to that child that sits alone... in fear of the hurt she has encountered. You are accepted, you are my child, and as the wind cradles this autumn leaf in change so My Spirit shall cradle and nurture you."*

At that moment, the presence of God was overwhelming and I saw Janice with tears in her eyes slowly overcome with incredible peace. Then as the Spirit of God was cradling her, she slid to the ground resting in the Spirit.

When she came to, she told me about some personal relationships she had and how the Lord was beginning to release her from bondage to this distorted self-image she had of herself. Since that time I have watched Janice truly blossom into a flower of sweet fragrance for the Lord.

In this situation, we see a similar pattern as our previous example. The Lord through this vision showed:

- Who needs prayer
- What the specific ailment was that need focus
- What action needed to be done to flow with the Spirit

He gave faith and hope, dispelling all fear to the one prayed for.

We also see from this example the Lord's heart towards inner healing. The mistake that we can make is assuming that what God desires to heal is that which we see with our natural eye. We need to be careful and listen to the Spirit of God - always seeking to collaborate with Him in what He is doing and not what we think needs to be done before we listen. It wasn't until after the healing of her self-image that her physical healing was manifest.

Proverbs 17:22 says: *"A merry heart does good, like medicine, But a broken spirit dries the bones."* It is clear from this verse that there can be a link between the wounded spirit or soul and physical illness. John, in 3 John 1:2, prays, *"Beloved, I pray that you may prosper in all things and be in health, just as your soul prospers."* He did not say "as your spirit prospers" but as your soul prospers. Again, the point is that a healthy soul can impact the state of your health.

Later we will discuss the Seer and inner healing but for now let me share with you another example that will expound on directional seeing.

An extension of My hands

In 1991, while working at CBN one of my employees had fallen and twisted her ankle. I walked in the office to see what happened and found her sitting in a chair with about eight to ten other employees standing around praying for her foot.

I immediately joined in with silent prayer. While I was praying, I felt this tremendous heat all over my hand. I placed my hand on the shoulder of one of the brothers praying, when he turned and said, "Boy your hand is really hot."

I responded praising God, saying, "The Lord's going to touch her." Then I saw a vision of beautiful meadow. Sitting on the grass of this meadow was this girl. Jesus was standing next to her. He bent over, grabbed her foot, and began praying for her. The serenity of this picture was truly tranquil.

Someone asked her if she had felt that the Lord was doing something. She said that her foot was still in pain. The group finished praying and one brother said, "Sister, we will just claim that healing for you." At that, they all returned to work.

Meanwhile, I was standing by her side, hands on fire and that vision of Jesus stuck in the forefront of my mind. I looked at April (her name) and said, "I think the Lord wants to heal your foot... I don't think we are really done praying yet."

I told April about the vision I had seen, and about the anointing, I had felt in my hands. Then the Lord said, "Fred, be an extension of my hands." That was when I understood that just as Jesus had bent down, held her foot, and began to pray, so in like manner he wanted me to do the same. I did and the warmth of His Spirit was all over April. God had healed her at that moment.

The reason this example is so crucial is here we see a team of brothers and sisters praying with all good intentions for April's healing. The problem was that the prayers went one way.... Nobody was really listening to what the Spirit was saying regarding her healing.

We as a people need to learn how to listen to the Spirit of God. We need to learn how to pray in team ministry. When we come together as members of the body of Christ in the process of ministering to an individual's needs we must understand that we are just that, members of His body. That collectively there will be a diversity of gifting. There needs to be a methodology in our ministry time. We need to fine-tune the way we pray for people in order to flow with the Spirit and not walk by Him while he desires to do something else. We need to get trained.

CHAPTER 5

Healing in General

"Along the bank of the river, on this side and that,
will grow all kinds of trees used for food; their
leaves will not wither, and their fruit will not fail.
They will bear fruit every month, because their
water flows from the sanctuary. Their fruit will
be for food, and their leaves for medicine."

- Ezekiel 47:12

"Moreover the word of the Lord came to me,
saying, Jeremiah, what do you see?
And I said, I see a branch of an almond tree. Then
the Lord said to me, You have seen well, for I am
ready to perform My word"

- Jeremiah 1:11-12

The Seer and Healing

Often times, the Lord, when giving information on a specific physical ailment, will give visions in the form of X-Rays. This kind of revelation is a good example of visions as the chosen language of God while receiving a "word of knowledge." It may take place any time during ministry. I have received this kind of revelation, many times, during worship. Let me share with you a few examples.

Illustrative Example

X-Ray

One Sunday a few years ago, I was attending a school of the Holy Spirit class at Vineyard Christian Fellowship in Virginia Beach. While in the midst of worship, the Lord showed me several pictures of what looked like X-Rays.

The first picture I received was the back inside view of a right ankle. As I looked I noticed that all the bones appeared to be intact except for a shadowy area on the inside ankle above the heel. Then the word "tendon" popped in my mind and I knew that the problem with this ankle was a torn or strained tendon and that nothing was broken.

The second picture I received was again a view from the backside, only this time it was the left shoulder blade or scapula bone. As I was staring at this picture, I felt a tremendous pain shooting through the shoulder and neck of this person. Then the thought came to my mind that this was related to muscle strain and possibly a pinched-nerve.

The third picture that came to my mind was the back view of a spinal column. I looked at the center of the spine and noticed a shadowy section closer to the thoracic vertebrae and the word growth popped into my mind. Then I saw a person-walking bent over like someone imitating an elephant. As I pondered this and asked the Lord what it meant, it came to me that this person was weighed down by this ailment, that the weight of this was crushing her spirit and her hope. It was as if she was caring excess baggage and the Lord wanted to take this away and heal her.

After I received these visions, I asked the Lord what he wanted me to do with them. All through the sermon, my prayers were ushered up the Father trying to get insight on the application of these visions.

The pastor finished his message and we immediately went into a time of ministry. Todd Hunter, my pastor, said that he believed that there were some people here that God wanted to heal. He asked if anyone had received anything from the Lord, please raise his or her hand.

While I was praying, I felt that I was only to share the one about the ankle. I raised my hand and shared that vision with the group. A man stood and said that the vision was for Him and that he had been experiencing pain in His right foot for several days now.

Todd asked those who had received revelation to come up and pray for those who responded to their word. As I began to pray for this man, the Lord kept showing me a picture of a screen door that kept opening and closing. As I shared with him this picture, I asked him if he had felt that the move of God in his life was inconsistent or if he felt he was having an unusual amount of dry spells. He responded with teary eyes and I knew he was weighed down by a performance or works attitude. I felt that the Lord wanted to refresh him with His Spirit and give him a new revelation of grace.

I asked him if I might stop praying for his foot and ask God to pour forth His Spirit and refresh this brother. He agreed and as I prayed, the Spirit of God moved on this brother in waves of refreshment. I stood back in amazement as God blessed this brother with His presence. After this time of out-pouring was over I prayed for his ankle and the Lord healed him.

You see, this brother had a roadblock in his mind, which was stopping him from receiving God's grace for his ankle. The Lord wanted to go to the root of the problem and work there before he moved with healing in His wings. This is very common in the ministry of healing. We must always seek the Lord for root revelation so that the Lord can lay the axe to the root of the tree... dealing with fruit that is bruised, blemished, or foreign.

As to the other two visions, I was puzzled that God had not released me to give those visions at that time. I was getting ready to leave when I saw a friend of mine standing nearby and went over to say hi. We chitchatted for a few minutes then he asked if I would join them in prayer for a friend of his. She had a pain in her shoulder and was visiting just for the night.

I asked Harry if it was her left shoulder and he said yes. I told them about the vision that I had seen and we started to pray for this woman. As I was praying, I felt a tremendous amount of heat all over my hand. I placed my hand on her shoulder and the heat intensified - the Lord was healing her shoulder.

I later found out that she wasn't very sure about the Lord's ability to heal in these days. She was taught that the gifts of the Holy Spirit had stopped at the end of the Apostolic-era. So here we see the wisdom of God in not embarrassing this woman publicly because, she probably would not have come forward resulting in no healing. I am sure that if I had shared this vision presumptuously to the whole group, this blessing would not have happened. It is very important for the person receiving revelation to move in wisdom's ways seeking God's application of the revelation and not assume that because you receive something it is to be shared with the whole group.

As to the final vision it was three days later that I meet the woman that this vision was for. That Wednesday I was asked to speak at chapel at CBNs afternoon service. CBN always rotates various speakers each day moving from one chapel to the other giving tremendous variety to the daily services. It was my turn to speak at the corporate support building and this was the largest and most exciting of all the chapels at CBN.

Prior to the service, the Lord impressed me to go throughout the chapel and lay hands on every chair in the room praying for everyone that would sit in the chair. I did this with great enthusiasm. My message that day would was on Jeremiah 17 verses 7-15, where I brought them to the point where they could cry out from their hearts verses 14 & 15:

> *"Heal me, O Lord, and I shall be healed; Save me, and I shall be saved, For You are my praise. Indeed they say to me, "Where is the word of the Lord? Let it come now!"*

As I got up to share this message the Spirit of God came on me very Suddenly, and that picture I had seen the other day flashed in front of my mind. I stood and began praising God for His mighty hand sharing with the crowd how God had impressed me to prayer for each chair in the chapel and that his desire was to touch each member of his body individually with a personal touch from his hand.

Then I shared that vision that I had received a few days earlier. A woman stood who had a lump on the center of her back. She said it was a tumor and she believed the vision was for her. A few people stood around her and we all began to pray for the healing of this tumor. The result of this was her complete healing.

A few days later, it was reported to me by the Chaplin, that several people had been healed at that service, including the woman with the tumor. Here again we see wisdom's ways in the exercise of gifts are the prerequisites to the successful outpouring of God's Spirit. If I had given this word prematurely on Sunday night, I might have discarded it due to the lack of response at Sunday night's service. Again, I say we have to listen, listen, and listen again.

As you can see, visions and dreams can play an important part in the ministry of healing. What is so exciting to me is the creative power of the Lord to speak to His children.

In endless ways, if we listen to the Lord and seek His face and not just His hand, we shall move out in greater dimensions of the Spirit than we have ever known before.

"But to you who fear My name, The Sun of Right-eousness shall arise, With healing in His wings; And you shall go out, And grow fat like stall-fed calves."

- Malachi 4:2

CHAPTER 6

Inner Healing

*"One thing I have desired of the Lord, That will I
seek: That I may dwell in the house of the Lord,
All the days of my life, To behold the beauty of
the Lord, And to inquire in His temple. For in the
time of trouble He shall hide me in His pavilion;
In the secret place of His tabernacle He shall hide
me; He shall set me high upon a rock.*

— Psalm 27:4, 5

*"Your ears shall hear a word behind you, saying,
'This is the way, walk in it.' Whenever you turn to
the right hand or whenever you turn to the left."*

— Isaiah 30:21

*"For in Him dwells all the fullness of the
Godhead bodily; and you are complete in Him,
who is the head of all principality and power."*

— Colossians 2:9,10

*"That He would grant you, according to the riches
of His glory, to be strengthened with might*

through His Spirit in the inner man, that Christ
may dwell in your hearts through faith; that you,
being rooted and grounded in love."

- Ephesians 3:16, 17

O ften, when one talks about inner healing, a red flag shoots up, on either side of the fence, proclaiming that, this kind of healing is valid, *or* that it is simply fantasy and has no place in the church today. Today, more than any other time in the history of the church, the need for inner healing to the body of Christ is critical. We, as a generation, are wounded, blinded by the weight of sins both past and present.

Many within the church are wounded vessels leaking out sap from the past. They build walls to shield their hurt or hide their pain. Their hearts are scabbed, driving them into stagnancy. This often causes them to run through the same recycled thought processes over and over again. Aspects of their lives are in zombie mode. They are driven by an unseen winds. This is often is due to an onslaught of sin and moral decay that oozes out of the culture we live in.

The effects are widespread, all we have to do is look around at the erosion on society, and we will see God's creation limping and staggering with the heaviness of sin's sludge dripping from every corner of our being. With drug abuse, sexual perversion, violence, abuse, occultism, and new age dabbling into the occult, it's no wonder that the majority of those brought in to the Kingdom of God, come in with excess baggage.

This onslaught of sin, affects every element of our being. It affects the lost and the save alike. Sin can plague bodies with sickness and addiction. Finely, it affects the soul or mind as seen in those who carry the pain of the past, and become psychologically bound by lies that replay in our thoughts like an old record player that constantly skips and replays. Sin affects the whole person, body, soul, and spirit.

Though some contend that man is a Dichotomy, (made up of two parts, body, and soul), this Dichotomous view falls apart in light of scripture and fails to recognize a distinction between the human soul and the human spirit. The scriptures make it very clear we are created as a Trichotomy; there is a distinction in our makeup. Take for example this passage from Hebrews.

> *"For the word of God is living and powerful, and sharper than any two-edged sword, piercing even to the division of soul and spirit, and of joints and marrow, and is a discerner of the thoughts and intents of the heart. And there is no creature hidden from His sight, but all things are naked and open to the eyes of Him to whom we must give account."*

> - Hebrews 4:12-13

It is evident from this passage; there is a division between the soul and the spirit. In fact, the Word of God has the power to divide these two natures of our being. The Greek word here for "powerful" is "energes," meaning: "energetic" or "actively at work," in this dividing and discerning process. Here the Holy Spirit shows us a parallel between the dividing of soul and spirit, and the dividing of joints and marrow, and thoughts & intents.

For just as the muscle moves joints and bones, carrying with them the marrow, which dwells helpless within the bone, so the thoughts of the soul drive the actions of the person while the intents of the spirit lay dormant within it. The writer of Hebrews shows us the power of the Spirit's ability to discern what is driven by the soul, compared to what is driven by the human spirit.

This whole dilemma is why Paul in Romans 5, 6, 7 & 8 struggles with the issues of overcoming the sinful nature of the flesh, or the sin infested soul. He went on to say that by putting the soul to death with the cross of Christ one could live in the new nature of the spirit (which was once dead, leaving man as a dichotomy) but is now alive in Christ Jesus (a resurrected spirit bringing about our trichotomous nature). This is further elaborated in another of Paul's writings where we read:

> "Now may the God of peace Himself sanctify you completely; and may your whole spirit, soul, and body be preserved blameless at the coming of our Lord Jesus Christ."

> - 1 Thessalonians 5:23

It is this process of sanctification that causes us to be transformed into the image of Christ (2 Corinthians. 3:17-18). Paul tells us in Romans:

> "And do not be conformed to this world, but be transformed by the renewing of your mind, that you

may prove what is that good and acceptable and perfect will of God."

- Romans 12:2

Renewing the mind is the process the Holy Spirit uses to replace the imprint of the world and replace it with the imprint of Christ Jesus. The mind has been programmed with natural "established attitudes." These are the beliefs, thoughts, ideas, opinions, convictions, and prejudices that we have concerning ourselves, others, objects, activities, and God. These can be formed by the influences from of our parents, the educational system, society (through books, television, movies, etc,) or religious training. These "established attitudes" become permeated with fleshly "personal interest" of selfishness and sinfulness. Because of these imprints, we act out, are driven by them, to achieve personal aspiration, gratification, and reputation, or we react through the fight, fright, or flight modality.

God knows our every thought. The mind needs to be renewed with Godly "established attitudes." When we are born again, we are a new creation. However, as John Wimber said:

> *"Everyone who comes to Christ, also come with all kinds of emotional and spiritual baggage. In some cases that baggage will make the job of spiritual formation extremely difficult. They come angry, confused, and bruised. Some of them have been chewed up and spit out by life's difficulties. Many people come from very nominal church background. They may mistrust the church. They may be individualistic,*

> *cocky, and arrogant when they walk in the
> door...."*

"Established attitudes" develop into a "mind-set" and these mind-sets drive the way we live and relate to the world around us. If our mind-set is healthy, our thoughts and attitudes are in alignment with the Word of God and His truth regarding our identity in Him. When this happens, our soul comes alive and we live through the truth of who we are in Christ. This process is called the renewing of the mind. Remember, "As a man thinks in his soul, so is he (in behavior)" (Proverbs 23:7).

If our mind-set is unhealthy (driven by lies), it will give us a false sense of identity, such as having a persona that is bent with an external orientation, e.g. "How I look," personal guilt through attitudes of worthlessness, or feeling inferior to others. The result is a person who may become self-conscious with an unhealthy desire to please others. We can become inundated with vain imaginations, fears, and phobias. The impact can result in attitudes of anger, impatience, hate, bitterness, resentment, revenge, suspicion, criticism, jealousy, un-forgiveness, blame, depression, co-dependency.

An unhealthy mind thinks differently about God. God may become irrelevant, archaic, and unnecessary or on the other extreme God may become "superstition" or "magical" - driving the individual into occult practices or witchcraft, leading to a demonic stronghold.

In Colossians we read:

> *"Therefore put to death your members which are on
> the earth: fornication, uncleanness, passion, evil de-*

sire, and covetousness, which is idolatry. ... Do not lie to one another, since you have put off the old man with his deeds, and have put on the new man who is renewed in knowledge according to the image of Him who created him, ... Therefore, as the elect of God, holy and beloved, put on tender mercies, kindness, humility, meekness, longsuffering;"

- Colossians 3:5, 9, 10, 12

Elsewhere we are commanded to put on the mind of Christ, in First Corinthians we read:

"For "who has known the mind of the Lord that he may instruct Him?" But we have the mind of Christ."

- 1 Corinthians 2:16

Look at these other verses in relationship to our minds.

"... be renewed in the spirit of your mind, and that you put on the new man which was created according to God, in true righteousness and holiness."

- Ephesians 4:23, 24

"Let this mind be in you which was also in Christ Jesus..."

- Philippians 2:5

"Therefore gird up the loins of your mind, be sober, and rest your hope fully upon the grace that is to be brought to you at the revelation of Jesus Christ;"

- 1 Peter 1:13

It is evident here there is a struggle going on within our members. The bible tells us that the flesh is at war with the spirit and the spirit with the flesh. It is this old nature popping out its ugly head, while we are in the midst of trying to walk in the spirit, which causes us to stumble and revert to our old nature. This was Paul's question in Romans:

> *"For we know that the law is spiritual, but I am carnal, sold under sin. For what I am doing, I do not understand. For what I will to do, that I do not practice; but what I hate, that I do. If, then, I do what I will not to do, I agree with the law that it is good. But now, it is no longer I who do it, but sin that dwells in me. For I know that in me (that is, in my flesh) nothing good dwells; for to will is present with me, but how to perform what is good I do not find. For the good that I will to do, I do not do; but the evil I will not to do, that I practice.*
>
> *Now if I do what I will not to do, it is no longer I who do it, but sin that dwells in me. I find then a law, that evil is present with me, the one who wills to do good. For I delight in the law of God according to the inward man. But I see another law in my members, warring against the law of my mind, and bringing me into captivity to the law of sin which is in my members. O wretched man that I am! Who will deliver me from this body of death? I thank God— through Jesus Christ our Lord!"*

> - Romans 7:14-25

Thank God, for Romans chapter eight for in it Paul sets out for us freedom from indwelling sin and the power of being sons of God. Look at the next few verses from Romans 8.

"There is therefore now no condemnation to those who are in Christ Jesus, who do not walk according to the flesh, but according to the Spirit. For the law of the Spirit of life in Christ Jesus has made me free from the law of sin and death. For what the law could not do in that it was weak through the flesh, God did by sending His own Son in the likeness of sinful flesh, on account of sin: He condemned sin in the flesh, that the righteous requirement of the law might be fulfilled in us who do not walk according to the flesh but according to the Spirit."

- Romans 8:1-4

Inner healing is dealing with the residue of our old nature, bringing it to death, that we may live and walk in the Spirit of the living God. The Holy Spirit is in effect rewiring our minds and creating new neurological pathways seeded in the word of God. This is healing of the soul.

When a child is abused and the thought of that pain is too unbearable to deal with, that child will plunge those memories into its sub-conscience mind just to survive, only to find out that throughout all their life they have been driven by unseen thought patterns. Whether they are driven by fear, loneliness, anger, or depression, in order for healing to come, there needs to be a point when they lay the axe to the root of that tree. Proverbs 18:14 says:

"The spirit of a man will sustain him in sickness, But who can bear a broken spirit?"

In Hebrews 12:15 we read:

> *"... looking carefully lest anyone fall short of the grace of God; lest any root of bitterness springing up cause trouble, and by this many become defiled;"*

The whole process of inner healing is to slay the grip and power that sin has on us. Healing of the physical body is distorting sins grip on a person physically in a given situation. This will ultimately take place at the resurrection and transformation of our bodies on the last day. Healing of the spirit is salvation, by being born again our spirits are quickened to life by His Spirit (1 Corinthians 6:17; 2 Corinthians 5:17). Inner healing is renewing our minds and healing our thought processes taking the axe to the hidden roots of destruction that dwell within us.

CHAPTER 7

Sozo

"Your ears shall hear a word behind you, saying, 'This is the way, walk in it,' Whenever you turn to the right hand or whenever you turn to the left."

- Isaiah 30:21

"Nor is there salvation in any other, for there is no other name under heaven given among men by which we must be saved (Greek: Sozo)."

- Acts 4:12

The Greek for *"being* saved" is "Sozo." It is used 110 times in the New Testament. It is an action/verb meaning *to be saved* or *rescued* out from under satan's power and to be restored into wholeness, body, soul, and spirit. It has been used to mean:

- Salvation (Acts 4:12; Romans 10:9; Ephesians 2:8).
- Healed from disease (Matthew 9:22; Mark 6:56; Mark 10:52).
- Delivered from demonic oppression (Luke 8:36; 2 Timothy 4:18; Jude 1:5).

- All three of these at the same time (Luke 1:9,10; John 20:21).

To be "sozo" is *to be saved through-and-through*, **saved**, **healed**, and **delivered**, from the clutches of the enemy, and set free in Christ as a new creation. Thank God, the sozo ministry has blossomed as it has today, much thanks to the ministry work of Bethel Church in Redding California. Dawna DeSilva's work in sozo ministry has spanned the globe in not only setting folks free but also equipping the church to carry the sozo torch.

I think it is so important to get a full understanding of this so that we can move out in wholeness and get on with the business of healing this dying world. Inner healing is part of the maturing process. It is not easy, but as Wimber has said:

> *"Christianity doesn't guarantee heaven here on earth. We're going to Heaven- But we may go through hell here on this earth! Maturity does not automatically come with the passage of years; some of the people we work with may be spiritually much younger than their chronological age. A prayer I pray often is: Lord, let me grow up, before I grow old."*

There are many wonderful books out there on the subject of inner healing and sozo. Dawna De Silva has written a dynamic series on the Sozo ministry, and I highly recommend her work (http://store.ibethel.org.

My purpose here is not to cover the vastness of inner healing. There are much more qualified individuals than myself that have taken up that task. My purpose is simply to show the relationship of visions and dreams in the ministry of inner healing.

Visions, Dreams, and the Ministry of Sozo

Visions and dreams can play an important role in the process of inner healing. God in a moment can cut asunder between soul and spirit showing us the root of the problem. He can also - to the one being healed - visually bring the truth of His love to a situation extinguishing the lies of the enemy with the light of His glory.

As a person moving in the inner-healing ministry, you will encounter a variety of problems. Following is a brief list to name a few.

- The healing of memories
- Shame
- Sexual brokenness
- Masculine/feminine soul identity
- Multiple personality disorders
- Satanic ritual abuse
- The healing of the wounded child
- Broken marital relationships
- The healing of inner vows
- The healing of bitter-root judgments
- Victims of violence
- Addictions
- The healing of cords of iniquity

The list goes on and on, changing with the challenges of every new generation. We are a complex creation in which only

Jesus can truly bring healing to our broken places. Jesus has come to set us free from the sin that weighs us down. He comes to take the pain from the past and like unraveling an onion he removes the layers of wounding that have resulted... laying an axe to the core of the problem.

Now let's look at some personal examples involving seeing and inner healing. I share these not to unload my personal history on you but to demonstrate the loving nature of Jesus Christ in the process of healing and to show examples of "how" the Lord uses visionary language to heal the inner man.

Illustrative Examples

Francis and Judith MacNutt

My first experience with inner healing came to me in 1986 at a healing conference sponsored by Vineyard Ministries International. It was held at the Anaheim Vineyard in Southern California. The team of speakers for the week included John Wimber, Francis MacNutt, and Judith MacNutt. Francis and Judith have a very special relationship to the ministry of healing and inner healing. As a team, they minister all over the world bringing the message of Jesus' power to heal, to millions.

On the forth night of the conference, Judith was speaking on rejection and the wounded child. At the end of her message, they called for a time of ministry to all in the auditorium. After a brief time of prayer and inviting the presence of the Holy Spirit to come, Judith began to sing in the Spirit. The power of that song was incredible, it sounded like a lullaby from Father God to my heart. Tears began to roll down my face and I went forward to get prayer.

During the prayer time, I was having a hard time trying to relax. Suddenly, the Lord showed me a vision. I saw my dad standing against a white background. It was as if I was looking at Him through the eyes of God. I saw him as a child. I saw the pain that he had inside and all the hurt and fear that was in his heart.

Then I saw Jesus standing next to him; he was looking at him with overwhelming love flowing out of Him. My dad was looking up at Him with eyes full of love and tears of pain, and joy. Then I saw the Lord take my father's heart and put it in His hand, and with both hands, He began to massage my father's heart. He was healing my father's heart.

I then saw the Lord take hold of my hand and put His hand on my heart. I felt as if I was getting heart surgery. Then He put my father and me together and I rested my head on my father's chest... as the Lord had his arms around the both of us. Tears began to run down my face and a weight was lifted from my heart.

Then I saw a vision of a hospital corridor, I was dressed in white and Jesus was by my side with His arm around me walking me back to my hospital room. The Lord spoke to me and said,

"That's all for now - but you know we're not finished."

When I came out of this trance, I felt like I was walking on air. His presence was so intense I felt a peace that was indescribable. The Lord had given me new eyes to see my father. He showed me how He saw my dad and that was life changing for me. A different kind of love was growing in my heart for my dad. A love that wasn't reactionary... I had always craved his love. I felt that somehow I had to earn it. Now I had a love of compassion. It was a deep love that didn't involve self-hunger... it was holy and pure, like a spring of water flowing from the thrown of God. Like the fulfillment of Malachi 4:6:

> *"And he shall turn the heart of the fathers to the children, and the heart of the children to their fathers, lest I come and strike the earth with a curse."*

I grew up sub-consciously feeling that I had to earn my father's love and that this love was conditional and fragile. This thought process not only affected our relationship but it also affected every area of my life because acceptance in general was based on performance. This was true even about my relationship with Jesus Christ.

At times, the struggle with this was overwhelming. In fact, all through this conference I kept telling the Lord that I wanted to see His face. I didn't want Him to leave me... I wanted to be as close to Him as I could possibly be. That night when I was leaving the conference, I walked to the car and sat in the front seat thinking about the events that had taken place.

Suddenly, the Lord spoke to me very clearly,

"Fred - Behold my Face."

I looked up in the sky and saw an open vision of the face of the Lord. I began to cry as waves of His love flowed through me.

Here we see how the Lord can use visions to reveal a truth about the one being prayed for. The visual symbolism of what He is doing awakens the soul to the light of His glory and cuts to the heart of the situation, laying an axe to the ties that bind. What is also interesting to me is that healing is a process, and the Lord is in no hurry to accomplish this. He chooses the right time and does no more than what needs to be done at that moment. The Lord is gentle when healing the damage of our fragile makeup, more so with inner healing than any other kind of healing.

I had been a Christian for seven years before the Lord began to work on that area of my life. With periodic intervals, God would work on healing my wounded spirit, yet it wasn't until the summer of 2010 that He would finish what he started in 1986. The Lord does not believe in premature healing - this could cause more damage than anticipated. We as ministers to the inner healing grace of the Lord Jesus Christ need to be very sensitive to the Spirit of God when we are ministering.

School Days

Another example from my own personal experience will help to shed some light on how the Lord uses visions to the person being healed in the ministry of inner healing.

In the autumn of 1989, I went through a time of intense inner healing. One night during a healing prayer session, the

Lord gave me a vision that opened a wound that was too deep to remember. In this vision, I saw myself walking besides an old stonewall. I came to a corner and turned to my right. In front of me on the right side there was a rod-Iron Gate enveloped by a fog. I stood paralyzed staring at this gate.

Then I saw Jesus walking up to me. He put His hand on my shoulder and asked me if I wanted to go inside. Fear struck my heart. I looked into His warm, gentle, reassuring eyes and said,

"I don't think I want to go in there."

The Lord asked me if I wanted to go for a walk. I took hold of His hand and together we went for a walk. We moved past the gate, still parallel with the wall. The Lord stopped and turned, putting the palms of His hands on the cheeks of my face. When He did this, I noticed that I had changed and turned into a child.

With youthful joy in the sound of His voice, He asked me if I wanted to play. I responded with hesitation, "Well O.K."

With that, I saw the Lord bend down and cup His hands to give me a boost over the wall. The next thing I knew we were running around this old park playing tag, hide & seek, and skipping stones across the stream. The serenity of this park was incredible. With weeping willows, rocks, tall grass, and a stream running through the center of the park we enjoyed the playful surroundings.

We stopped and began to walk along the stream. As we were walking, we came to an area that was enclosed in fog. I stopped at the edge of the fog not wanting to walk any further. Then Jesus looked into my eyes and said,

"It's ok, I will be with you - I will clear the way."

As I walked towards the fog, my heart pounding uncontrollably, I noticed the fog beginning to clear. I continued to walk and Suddenly, found myself on a school playground standing by a tetherball pole. I was five years old and the memory of what had taken place at school started to come back to me.

I saw myself reenacting the event only this time I knew that Jesus was with me. When I was five years old, I went to a private school in Southern California. This uniformed school was very strict on discipline.

One day I got to school late. Not realizing that I was late, I stopped to play tetherball on the playground before class. I wondered where all the kids were, not thinking that school had already started.

When I got to my room, the teacher was very upset. She asked me where I've been. I told her I was playing tetherball. She then grabbed my arm and said - you're going to the hallway. When she said that I started to cry telling her I didn't want to go.

The hallway ran along the back of all the classrooms. It was a place where they stored boxes and chairs and it was the back entrance to the rooms. This hallway was also the place that they put kids to be spanked with a wooden paddle. The hallway had very poor lighting and on the right side of the door in the hallway was a chair that kids who were being punished would sit and wait.

The janitor was assigned to the spanking detail. Jesus brought me back to this classroom. I saw the door that led to the hallway. Fear struck me when Jesus asked me if I was ready to go in there. Then He said that He would go in first and nothing would happen to me because He was with me.

The Lord opened the door and walked in. I clung to His robe and slowly walked in behind Him. He put me in that little chair and stood between the darkness and me. I then heard the sound of a paddle moving across some boxes like the sound one would make if they were running a stick along the side of a fence while they were walking.

I got very scared and started to cry. Jesus turned and wiped the tears from my eyes saying,

> *"It's ok. I'm with you and nobody is going to hurt you."*

I felt a peace come over me. As I looked down that dark hallway, listening to the sound of that paddle against the wall, all of a sudden, the sound stopped and I saw a little man on his hands and knees cowering on the floor moving towards Jesus. It was as if he was trying to hide his face from the light of the Lord.

Jesus turned and looked at me,

> *"Is this the man that hurt you?"*

The tears began to flow again as I responded, "He's the one - he did it!"

Jesus turned and said to me,

"You know what you have to do now don't you?"

"Yes Lord - I do..." With my voice all choked up and pain in my heart I looked at him and said, "I forgive you for what you did to me."

I then saw this man move back in shame to the darkness and disappear. I started to cry even harder. Then Jesus picked me up and held me close to Him taking my pain into Himself.

Jesus was beginning to heal the brokenness in my heart. I had replaced the childhood joy of playing with performance for acceptance. The Lord was starting to restore playfulness to that wounded child within me... healing me from the fear of having fun. At that time the Lord never really showed me exactly what this man did in that dark hallway to me. That was a time of healing just one layer of an onion. I would not really experience the fullness of healing until I dealt with the root of what was really happening.

All through this vision it was as if I was a spectator to the events that had taken place. This detachment had its roots in **"Shame"** the act of "*cutting off*" a facet of one's self. In this case, I had cut out that child within me from myself. It wouldn't be until during the preparation of this manuscript and a sozo session I had in 2010 that the Lord began to show me the extent of the damage and heal another layer in that onion, a layer of sexual brokenness in my life. For this man, spanking was a pleasure. What he did in the midst of this punishment I still find hard to discuss. It was during that session that I was fully restored and was also healed in my relationship with Poppa God.

I thank the Lord for His patience in healing. I thank the Lord that this is an ongoing work of wholeness and that the gentleness of His workmanship makes the healing process worth it.

What this man did was inexcusable. However, God had to free me from the hate and the fear of what this man had done to a five-year-old boy. The result of the pain was self-hatred of that child within. I disassociated myself with that part of me. Shattered innocence seems to be a trademark that the enemy loves to use in the sick and perverted days in which we live. How many people are there that are bound up by the brokenness of abuse and victimization? Who hide behind stonewalls they set up in their lives, afraid to enter the fog from the past. Like medieval dungeons in the basements of our minds, we hear the horrifying echo of the past crying out to haunt us. Notwithstanding, to the Lord these are root cellars and he has come to lay the axe at the root of the pain that haunts us. Christ has come to set us free. He has come to bring health and life to the broken places of our past in order that our present can be fruitful and that we may be partakers in the healing of others in the future.

When I was in prayer asking the Lord to heal the shame in me, the Lord spoke to my heart and said,

> *"Fred are you willing to go into this memory as an adult and face you, as a child?"*

I told the Lord that I was willing to do this. When I had said that the Lord gave me a vision of that memory and I was standing in the hallway facing this child that was sitting in the chair scared and trembling. I was yelling at the child. "I hate you for what you did! - Why did you do that? It's all your fault... If you hadn't been playing nothing would had happened. What's wrong with you? You're a stupid, stupid child... I don't like you at all! I hate what you did to me! You are no longer my friend I want no part of you!"

As I was looking at myself yelling at this child, I could feel the hatred that I had for him... for myself. I could feel it in my heart.

Then the Lord spoke to me and said,

> "Fred... Don't you see... this is sin...? What you are doing is sin."

"I KNOW... it hurts so much," then I started to cry, "Lord please forgive me for hating this child; Please forgive me for hating me."

When I had finished saying this, the presence of the Lord was all over me and I knew that he had forgiven me. All I could do was cry, thanking Him repeatedly.

Then the Lord spoke to me,

> "Ask this child to forgive you for hating him. Self hatred is cancerous to your soul."

I was back in this memory standing before this child. I was worn down... emotionally wiped... as I looked at this little boy sitting scared in the chair.

"Please...." The tears began to flow again, as I tried to seek his forgiveness. "Please forgive me for hating you and abandoning you."

This little boy kept holding out his hand to me with tears rolling down his checks. "I forgive you.... It wasn't my fault you know.... It really wasn't. I just didn't know what to do I was so scared."

Then the Lord spoke to me and asked me,

> *"What does this child need from you?"*

I said, "He wants me to hold him and never leave him again."

> *"Are you willing to do this?"*

"Yes Lord I think I'm ready."

The next thing I saw was Jesus standing between this child and me. He held out His hand towards me and gently pulled me towards this child. With His other hand, He lifted this child from His seat and brought Him to me. With His arms around the both of us He looked up to heaven, his face began to glow, and He cried,

> *"Father I thank you for your tender mercy. I thank you that your love endures forever - now Father I pray that these two may be as one even as we are one."*

As He said these words, His hands began to glow and the brightness of His being filled the vision that I was seeing. He was merging the two of us together. Then I saw myself kneeling before the Lord and this child was glowing from my heart with his head bowed worshiping in like manner.

Then I saw myself at the Lord's feet. My tears were rolling down my face and onto the feet of the Lord. He reached down, picked me up, and wiped away the tears from my face. As he picked me up, I could see the child within me. The Lord held me and said,

> *"I have not rejected you... for I am in you and you are in Me... I love you with an everlasting love."*

When this was over, I just sat there and cried.

Sozo - My Love encounter with the Godhead

I would like to close this chapter on the seer and inner healing with a sozo story from my journal, summer, 2010. I wrote this log entry after a Sozo session conducted by Dawna De Silva.

6/11/10

The Lord has been doing a lot of healing in my heart the last three months. And this last week the Lord was working overtime on areas in my life, dealing with my ability to accept his unconditional love. Four days ago, I had a breakthrough with the Lord and He had released such peace in my heart – I could not believe it. The knot in my chest that kept driving me into His healing arms was gone; it had been replaced with peace. Even my breathing changed. He had taken me to a place and was dealing with an issue that had governed my life from the time I was born. He brought me back to some milestones in my life....

He flooded my mind with memories. I remembered when he had started healing this thing, 15 years earlier, at Vineyard in Virginia Beach, when He brought me back to my birth. He told me, he was there the day I was born: When, Suddenly, I was back there in a little 1950s kitchen, my Mom dressed in 50s style cloths with her dark red lipstick and fire red hair. She was so much younger than I had thought and she was pregnant. She was wearing an apron. The scene flashed forward and she was lying on the floor, in pain. Jesus was there in that kitchen, He was kneeling over my mother with his hand on her stomach. She was going into premature delivery. She had been injured, like she was kicked in the stomach. Hours later, Jan 4, 1957, I was born, 3 lb, 8 oz. and was three months a preemie.

Jesus said,

> *"I have always been with you and I will always be available to you. I was there when they thought you would not live – when you came out... I saw a boxer..."*

He was pointing out all the places of death and destruction in my life, when my Nana passed away. He was there. He was with when my parents were torn apart. He was with me when my little brother tried to kill himself.... All these memories kept flooding my mind. He was with me when my older brother Bobbie died... and he walked with me when cancer took my mother and she went to be with Jesus. Then he said:

> .... And yes, Fred, I was there with you in your great sadness, the day your son passed away. I will always be there with you. I will always be your comfort and your rear guard. I will never leave you, nor forsake you; I have got you in the palm of my hands...

He explained to me how the "**spirit of death**" had governed my life and that He was cutting off the cords of death from me and bringing me into life. I never knew it. I had never seen it. I knew that something had governed my life not to believe. I knew that deep inside I was not accepted but I didn't know why. It was destructive but I could never put my finger on it.

However, now it all began to make sense, I was starting to understand. The spirit of death had tried to rob me from life and from my destiny in Christ. The Lord in that moment had embraced my heart, something broke inside, and I knew I was free, and I began to cry.

Then, the last two days, Jesus kept telling me,

> "What I show you – I am going to do."

Over, and over He kept saying it. All day long I would hear him saying,

> "What I show you, I AM going to do."

I got so excited when I heard Him say it. I was thrilled at the thought of Him doing what He said He was going to do.

Then the night before last, He said,

> *"Fred, do you believe I am going to do what I show you?"*

It struck me in the heart. I was struggling with this so much. He kept asking me, repeatedly. The knot returned, and I groaned inside. I said, "Lord, I thought we were done? I thought we had taken care of the healing I needed?" In a panic, I went back to my Sozo sessions, trying to find something, anything, to heal my unbelief and bring release to this knot in my chest, but could not. I told the Lord I was going to bed.

In the morning when I woke up, I heard the Holy Spirit singing this song to me:

> *"Come up... here.... ...come up.. here ... ...come up.. here ... ...Where I am...."*

And I knew what he wanted me to do.

With all my heart, I wanted to move into a place of healing. I was hungry for a touch, to be released. In my heart was the deep desire to have intimacy with the Lord, to go deeper and get as close as possible to Him. I wanted healing, on the inside, of those things that were hindering me from going deeper and having that close – very close relationship with Poppa.

It was about 5:00 AM when I started worshiping the Lord. Shortly thereafter, I decided to continue a Sozo session by Dawna De Silva. I wanted to go deeper with the Godhead. I wanted to allow Jesus to heal me some more. Dawna was walking us through the doorways to the heavenly realm. In that moment, The Lord brought me to a heavenly place. This is what the Lord showed me...

Jesus

As I began to focus on the Lord, I saw Him walking on the beach towards me, smiling. I asked Him a simple question, "Jesus, what do you think of me?"

He smiled tenderly,

> *"I love you so very much. You are the apple of my eye, my soul's delight. You are my friend and I love you dearly. I love being with you."*

I felt his unconditional love for me and it drew me in. It felt so natural. So I thought I would ask him another question, "Jesus, what do you want to show me? Show me that special place."

He took a hold of my hand; we turned, and started to walk. Suddenly, I was standing in heaven, by the river of life. Jesus was standing next to me. He was filled with kindness and Joy. I could sense that He was full of mystery and wonder.

Then He smiled and said,

> *"Come, let's go for a walk."*

I felt as if I was walking with my best friend. Joy and acceptance filled my heart. Along the bank of the river were pillars. They were ancient pillars, covered with moss and growth.

Jesus said,

> *"These are the pillars of faith. Come let's walk amongst them."*

So we walked between the pillars and talked as we walked. I was staring at them, looking at the care and craftsmanship of their design, their age, and the life that covered them. As we walked, we headed towards the river's edge – to the water line. The river was very peaceful, like a lazy river, like you would see down south, in the delta marshland. Trees surrounded the river with hanging air moss and vines draping down. The place was full of life. Jesus pointed to the plants and the flowers. There was fruit everywhere. It was as if all the foliage, and the bugs, and bees, butterflies and frogs, all worshiped God.

Jesus rolled up His pant legs. He was barefoot. He said,

> *"Come on, let's go in."*

So I rolled up my pants, took off my shoes, and stepped into the water. It was cool and refreshing.

He said,

> *"Oh – doesn't that feel good..., the cold mud between your toes?"*

"Yea," I said, "it feels GREAT."

He smiled. He kept pointing life out. A golden fish popped up through the water. Jesus said,

> *"Look, look, over there. What a great catch!"*

I was watching that gold fish with its massive gills swimming at the surface of the water. I was amazed at the mystery of it all.

We stepped out of the water. Jesus pointed over to a horizon at the bend of the river. In front of the horizon was a mighty archway. He said,

> *"See the horizon? It was there, just beyond the edge of heaven that I saw you. Before time and space, I called you forth. I was with you the day you were conceived. I have always been with you and have always loved you. You are my hearts delight. I love you Fred. I desire to be with you and to walk, and talk with you. This is so good, isn't it?"*

"Yes Lord, this is very good."

Then He pointed to the horizon, to the archway and said,

> *"Look, your destiny... it's just around the bend."*

I could feel his love pouring over me. I was captured by His love for me.

Then He took my hand, and said,

> *"Come, let me take you to the Father."*

My heart was in my throat. It was starting to beat fast, as if I was fearful to see Him. I was wrestling with this on the inside. Jesus squeezed my hand. I was so comfortable with Jesus. I knew He loved me deeply and that I was His friend. But the father, that was a little different. We were walking up a road headed to what looked like a castle or something. The landscape had changed. It was like rolling hills with incredible blue and cloud studded white sky.

It almost looked like a scene from the wizard of Oz heading to emerald city.

Poppa

Then all of a sudden, Jesus was gone. I front of me was Poppa, though I could barely make him out. He was so big and swirling around like massive clouds. Then he stopped and I could make out His eyes upon me. Goodness and Joy started to fill the air. I looked up at Him and asked Him a question, "Father, are you pleased with me?"

In a moment, He was in front of me. All I could see was His chest. Hanging around His neck was a beautiful chain with a gold locket around it. He opened the locket and inside there was a picture of me, I was over taken by Him. He showed me His heart. He said,

"My heart beats for you. I crafted you and created you. I love every part of you. All your hairs are numbered. Every day has been treasured in my Heart."

I saw this big animated heart, pumping and beating. It was almost funny, and the father smiled and said,

"I love you so deeply. Did you know that before you were born; before the universe was even created, I dreamed of you? Yes, it's true; I saw you before the earth was formed. I have loved you from the moment I dreamed you into my heart. You are the apple of my eye."

Then I saw a big book open, and I understood it to be the days of my life. I saw the Father reading the book and turning the pages, as if He was enjoying every moment, as if He was reading a photo album. Then, I saw myself standing before the throne of God and I was dressed in royal attire, bowing before His throne. Then the Father said,

> *"This is what I saw the day I created you. This is what I saw the day you were born." He smiled."*

He took me to the pier in Bahia Beach Florida. The day after my son had died. I was standing at the end of the pier crying out to God. "Why, Why...?" I cried, all night long – My heart was broken.

Suddenly, I saw the Father there at that place, and He wrapped His arms around me and said,

> *"I know how much it hurts. I love you, and JJ is with me. I love you let Me comfort you.... You know I am for you, and I am with you, I am with you all the time. I will never leave you nor forsake you; I have you in the palm of My hands."*

I could feel the Father's love. I was starting to warm up to Him. So I asked him a question, "Poppa, what gifts do you want to give me...?"

At that moment, I was overwhelmed by Poppa's eagerness. I saw Him reach out and place a gold and red crown on my head. He took a golden scepter with a large diamond tip, and placed it in my hands. I was overwhelmed. Then He stood me up. It was like we were standing in front of all the kingdom of heaven. Around, everywhere you could look were heavenly palaces and it felt like a mystical wonderful place – full of life!

He stood with a smile on His face. His joy filled the kingdom like the wind of God. He had in His hand a glorious red robe. He cried out in a load voice, as if He was making announcement, like He was presenting me to the nations and to the Kingdom of Heaven,

"This is my beloved Son, in whom I AM very well pleased."

Then He draped the robe over my shoulders, and I stood there and cried. Poppa accepted me. He loved me, He approved of me. Something inside of me broke. I looked in His eyes and saw Poppa – and **I knew He adored me....**

Then, as I looked deeper into His eyes, I could see my eyes – looking into the eyes of others – showing them the Love of Poppa.

Then Poppa Said,

"I want to introduce you to someone... to the Holy Spirit."

I said, "Thank you Poppa for revealing your presence to me... for showing me how much you love and accept me. Poppa, thank you for setting me apart and loving me. Thank you for knowing my name."

The Holy Spirit

Suddenly, I was in a whirlwind. The whirlwind was full of color, like the colors of fire and sunset. We were spinning around faster, and faster. When I stopped, I felt this incredible laughter fill the place. I could hardly recognize the Holy Spirit, but I felt Him, and that I knew Him. He was almost funny and playful. I stopped and asked the Holy Spirit, "What do you want to impart to me?"

Suddenly, I saw myself standing in front of the Holy Spirit with my hands held out. The word "*Apostle*" was written on my left hand and the word "*Prophet*" were written on my right hand. I stood back and wondered. I looked down at my feet, on the topside of both of feet were written the words "*Healing.*" I looked down at my chest and I saw my heart. As I looked, it began to enlarge and expand in my chest. Golden oil began to flow from my heart and it was pouring onto other people. Then the Holy Spirit said to me,

> *"Look, learn how to use your robe...."*

I saw the Holy Spirit with my robe in His hands, He walked up to a body of water and struck the water with the robe, and it parted. Then I saw a storm coming in and the Holy Spirit held up the robe and quieted the storm. Then I saw Him take the robe and drape a family that was shivering in the cold. Then He said,

> *"Your robe can be a vessel of peace and of comfort."*

Then He said,

> *"Look, this is how you use your scepter."*

The diamond on the tip of the scepter began to shoot out beams of white light. The Holy Spirit took the scepter, He swung it like a sword, and it opened up the heavens. He swung it again and it cut into the hearts of men opening them up for the Poppa's touch. He swung it again and rivers of water burst through the earth. Then He said,

"The Diamond glimmers with the nature of God, and it cuts through things like a laser... it becomes His eyes in the hands of one walking in authority."

Then He said,

"Go and learn what has been given you. Stir up the deposit and the gifting in your life. Understand your inheritance and your place in the kingdom of God."

Suddenly, I felt as if I was basting in warm golden oil. When I opened my eyes, I saw all three together in perfect joy, unity, peace, and complete happiness. As I looked at them, I was overwhelmed with how much they truly loved me. The whole experience was about an hour maybe more – but it seemed to be eternal. Thank you Jesus, Thank you Poppa, and Thank you Holy Spirit – I love you!

End of Journal entry...

Healing of relationship with the Godhead is a powerful thing. As you can see, inner healing and God's ability to communicate through visions are very closely related. The Lord also uses visions within the ministry of inner healing in the context of words of knowledge, which we will discuss later. This is information given to a member of the prayer team or counselor about the individual receiving ministry. Now let

me close with the following Scriptures, expressing the heart
of the God we serve:

> *"There shall come forth a Rod from the stem of Jesse, And a Branch shall grow out of his roots. The Spirit of the Lord shall rest upon Him, The Spirit of wisdom and understanding, The Spirit of counsel and might, The Spirit of knowledge and of the fear of the Lord. His delight is in the fear of the Lord, And He shall not judge by the sight of His eyes, Nor decide by the hearing of His ears; But with righteousness He shall judge the poor, And decide with equity for the meek of the earth; He shall strike the earth with the rod of His mouth, And with the breath of His lips He shall slay the wicked. Righteousness shall be the belt of His loins, and faithfulness the belt of His waist."*

> *- Isaiah 11:1-5*

> *"The Spirit of the Lord GOD is upon Me, Because the Lord has anointed Me To preach good tidings to the poor; He has sent Me to heal the brokenhearted, To proclaim liberty to the captives, And the opening of the prison to those who are bound; To proclaim the acceptable year of the Lord, And the day of vengeance of our God; To comfort all who mourn, To console those who mourn in Zion, To give them beauty for ashes, The oil of joy for mourning, The garment of praise for the spirit of heaviness; That they may be called trees of righteousness, The planting of the Lord, that He may be glorified."*

> *- Isaiah 61:1-3*

This is the mighty Lord that we serve, the healer of our body, soul and spirit, Amen!

CHAPTER 8

Healing of the Demonized

*"And these signs will follow those who believe: In
My name they will cast out demons; they will
speak with new tongues; they will take up
serpents; and if they drink anything deadly, it will
by no means hurt them; they will lay hands on
the sick, and they will recover."*

- Mark 17:17-18

I cannot dive into the subject of healing without touching upon the Seer and his relationship to healing those bound by the demonic. If you have spent any amount of time praying for those in need, chances are you have, or will, encounter the demonic. When such an encounter takes place, our call is simple: to bind the strongman, proclaim liberty to the captives, and set the prisoners free. Historically we have called this form of ministry "deliverance." It is vitally important for us to have a solid understanding of this ministry. We are living in a time when the hearts and minds of people are under assault like never before. Of course, this is and has always been satan's plan. Yet, today, we are seeing the stage set for a massive increase in his assault on humanity.

In the last fifty years, in western society, we have seen a blending of occult, Eastern mysticism, and materialistic secular humanism that has created, not an organized religion, but a sub-culture or network of individuals, that have penetrated every aspect of society into what is referred to as the "New Age" movement.

This new spiritual or religious humanism commingles the worship of self and the evolutionary id with Eastern or occult powers and pseudoscience. The goal is simple, if secularization wants to crowd God out of the cosmos, the new secularization, represented by the new age, encourages people to equate God with the cosmos – all is god – we are all god. The new age movement is an exceedingly large, loosely structured, network of organizations and individuals bound together by common values - based in mysticism and monism (the worldview that "all is one" and a common vision). This vision is the coming of a "new age" of peace and mass enlightenment, or the "age of Aquarius."

When we pull back the curtain, we see satan and his horde of minions working behind the scenes to bring about this movement. As this cultural shift takes hold and the new age becomes mainstream we can expect a massive rise in individuals being exposed to the demonic realm. This exposure is an open door to demonic possession or oppression. Our job is the same as Jesus, to destroy the works of the devil and set the captives free, for we are His body here on earth.

Our warfare is not against flesh and blood. People are victims, no matter the cause. Paul tells us very clearly in the book of Ephesians that our warfare is against satan and his principalities, powers, rulers of the darkness of this age, and the spiritual hosts of wickedness in heavenly places. This includes ruling fallen angels and demonic evil spirits.

> *"Finally, my brethren, be strong in the Lord and in the power of His might. Put on the whole armor of God, that you may be able to stand against the wiles of the devil. For we do not wrestle against flesh and blood, but against principalities, against powers, against the rulers of the darkness of this age, against spiritual hosts of wickedness in the heavenly places."*

- Ephesians 6:10-12

The deception of mainstream humanism muddies the waters of clarity as it relates to the occult. Historically, open occultism was easy to spot, but now, thanks to the saturation of the new age movement in society, more and more people have opened the doors to the demonic without realizing it.

My own personal experience with the occult makes this chapter an important part of this book. You see, in my family, the door to the occult world opened up a hundred and thirty years before the current mysticism movement. My family was bound by the cult of spiritism, and stayed bound for generations, until the Lord drew a line in the sand.

For years, gaining information from the world beyond, communication with the dead (also known as necromancy), and seeking relationship with un-seen entities, plagued my Dad's side of the family. According to my father, my great grandmother was a medium when the spiritism revival first took place in the 1880's. This was the beginning of my family's involvement in spiritism.

The only spiritual influence I had as a child came from spiritism, table moving, and communication with the dead. This was my religion. My Aunt Eva was a powerful medium, she would barely touch a table, and the so-called spirits would be summoned. When I was a kid, my Uncle Bud used to chase us around the backyard of my Aunt's house, by moving wooden picnic benches with only his fingertips touching the tops of the bench. This scared the heck out of me, but at the same time, growing up, I wanted to do that, to be just like my Aunt. There seemed to be so much power in it.

Who were these spirits? I was taught as a child, that they were departed loved ones. In this chapter, I will not only answer that question, but also show you how the Holy Spirit uses the Word of knowledge via the Seer's gift in ministry to the demonized, and show how you can be an effective minister in setting free those that are bound. At the end of this book, I share my personal story and how Jesus set me free from the demonic stronghold that bound my life.

The pursuit of the occult and speaking to the spirit world is rooted in the prideful pursuit for revelation, knowledge, power, and control. As we have seen throughout this book, the secret to revelation is not revelation, its relationship. It does not come through satanically dabbling in the occult. Behind that door lies lying revelation and bondage to demons. True revelation is birthed out of a relationship with the Son of God. It is the "out-flow" of fellowship with Jesus

Christ and his Word. To begin this chapter we will start by lying out some foundational truths.

Foundational Truths

We are in a war!

Most Christians never consider the fact that at the heart of the incarnation of Christ was the defeat of satan (1 John 3:8). It is critical to understand this. Everything in this book revolves around that one truth: We are sent to release the captives and set the prisoners free so that their eyes could be opened and they could see the light of our glorious Lord. Our job is to take back the territory that the enemy has seized and usher in the kingdom of God, leaving out this essential truth from gospel message runs in direct conflict with the mission of Jesus Christ. If we are going to be successful in our quest as Christians, this truth must be front and center in all that we do!

Salvation is nothing less than God rescuing humanity from the grip of satan and restoring us into relationship with the living God. Only when we are freed from his grip can we see the truth. You see, once we recognize satan's role in keeping people in darkness, we will awake with a new sense of urgency to bind the works of the enemy, heal the sick, raise the dead, and cast out demons from those that are bound.

demons are satan's foot soldiers. They have one role in the kingdom of darkness: to keep people in darkness. They achieve this goal by invading people's lives and binding them to circumstances or situations through lies and sins until their condition seems to be greater than God's ability and power to forgive and redeem them, leaving victims that feel lost, brutalized, and worn down with no hope of recovery. Due to satan's grip they have become blind to the light of the world, Jesus Christ.

Jesus gave us a clear commission to combat the work of demons when He said:

> *"And these signs will follow those who believe: In My name they will cast out demons;..."*

> *- Mark 16:17*

We can see this reinforced in the commission of the apostle Paul after Christ's ascension:

> *"I will deliver you from the Jewish people, as well as from the Gentiles, to whom I now send you, to open their eyes, in order to turn them from darkness to light, and from the power of satan to God, that they may receive forgiveness of sins and an inheritance among those who are sanctified by faith in Me.'"*

> *- Acts 26:17-18*

I find it so very sad that the world wanders around in the dark; oblivious that satan is the god of their reality and is ruling them with his power. People are not able to "receive forgiveness of sins," without being set free from satan's grasp, demonized or not. To illustrate this truth I will use the action movie, the "Matrix" to illustrate. In this movie, we see the following:

- Computer hacker Neo (pre-Christian in need of salvation)
- Is contacted by underground freedom fighters (Christians engaged in the battle to set the captives free)
- Who explain that reality as Neo understands it (this worlds system) is actually a complex computer simulation called the Matrix (world under satan's rule).
- Created by a malevolent Artificial Intelligence (satan), the Matrix hides the truth from humanity, allowing them to live a convincing (life is good, there is no God, there is no devil), simulated life while machines (demons) grow and harvest people to use as an ongoing energy source.
- The leader of the freedom fighters, Morpheus (the Holy Spirit), believes Neo is "The One" (us, as the body of Christ) who will lead humanity to freedom and overthrow the machines (demonic and works of the devil.)
- Together with Trinity (you get the picture), Neo and Morpheus fight against the machine's enslavement of humanity.

Truthfully, the only reason people remain in their sins is due to the dark forces that keep them blinded to the truth. Their unbelief is not caused by God's unwillingness to awaken them to the truth. On the contrary, God wants all to come to the saving knowledge of the grace found in Jesus Christ (2 Peter 3:9).

The good news is that Christ has given us the authority and power to bind the devil and stop him in his tracks from blinding the spiritual eyes of nonbelievers. He has sent us out as laborers in a field ripe for harvest (Matthew 9:38) and equipped us with His power and authority to accomplish the task.

Our job: to use the authority and power Christ has given us and stop the enemy for stealing the Word from people's hearts (Luke 8:12). We do this by binding him. When we tell him to stop, he must obey. We turn people from the power of satan's rule by binding his efforts and preaching the gospel to them. This is a battle for the souls of humanity. We are the answer the world is looking for, and God is sending us into the harvest.

It's not just the lost!

> *"But I fear, lest somehow, as the serpent deceived Eve by his craftiness, so your minds may be corrupted from the simplicity that is in Christ."*

> - 1 Corinthians 11:3

Why was Paul concerned about the Church at Corinth? Certainly, he was not one easily given to fear. Something was troubling him. Why was he troubled? He feared that satan was leading the church away from the pure and simple devotion to Christ. The enemy's tactics have not changed; they are the same as they were in the garden: to fog, distort, twist, cause confusion, and remove the truth of God's Word from your heart. Deception is a powerful weapon. If satan can cause you to question God's motives, the next logical step is for him to rob you of the Word spoken into your life. He wants to rob you of your identity in Christ and sabotage your destiny.

Yet, Paul says, "for we are not ignorant of his devices (2 Corinthians 2:11)." The point is, we need to be cognizant of his devices to be effective at waging this war against him. Too many Christians lose the battle with satan because they are ignorant of his plan to destroy their walk with God. The devil will use everything at his disposal to accomplish that end. He is ruthless in his assault. He is cunning and patient, lying in wait for the opportune time, while he weaves a web of entrapment to deceive and cause you to stumble.

Of course, sin is one of satan's most powerful weapons. He uses deception as a means to coerce a person to sin. It's ironic, the devil drives us to sin, and then condemns us for the sin he tempted us to do. It's the same old story. Yet, little did he know, God's plan was to take away our sins and remove all condemnation.

If we get a hold of the fact that:

- We are in an ongoing war for the souls of humanity.
- Jesus has defeated ALL the power and authority of the enemy on the Cross.
- We as believers have the righteousness of Christ as members of His body.
- We have been given the same power and authority in Christ, to overcome the enemy.
- We have been commissioned by Jesus to bind the strongman and take back what is rightfully His.

- Our warfare is not against flesh and blood, but against the powers of darkness.

Then, when these truths settle in our spirits, we will arise with new vigor and might, and take our position as princes in the household of God. Only then can we begin to be effective in our ministry to the lost and demonized.

Before we discuss the ministry of the demonized, I want to discuss briefly the nature of heaven and clarify the difference between angels, fallen angels, and demons.

CHAPTER 9

Heaven, Angels, and the Demonic

*"For we do not wrestle against flesh and blood,
but against principalities, against powers, against
the rulers of the darkness of this age, against
spiritual hosts of wickedness in the heavenly
places"*

- Ephesians 6:12

*"It is doubtless not profitable for me to boast. I
will come to visions and revelations of the
Lord: I know a man in Christ who fourteen
years ago—whether in the body I do not
know, or whether out of the body I do not
know, God knows—such a one was caught up
to the third heaven. And I know such a man—
whether in the body or out of the body I do not
know, God knows— how he was caught up into Paradise and heard inexpressible words,
which it is not lawful for a man to utter. Of
such a one I will boast; yet of myself I will not
boast, except in my infirmities. For though I
might desire to boast, I will not be a fool; for I
will speak the truth. But I refrain, lest anyone
should think of me above what he sees me to
be or hears from me."*

- 2 Corinthians 12:1-5

The Hebrew word for "heavens" is "shamayim," it is plural word meaning "heights," or "elevations." It is found in the first verse of Genesis chapters one and two. The Bible speaks of three heavens. Paul refers to being caught up to the third heaven also called Paradise (2 Corinthians 12:2-4). The fact that Paul describes a third heaven implies that a third heaven cannot exist without a first and second.

The first heaven refers to the atmospheric area of the fowl (Hosea 2:18) and clouds (Daniel 7:13). The second heaven is the area of the stars and planets (Genesis 1:14-18). It is also the abode of all supernatural angelic beings. The Scriptures tell us that there are two locations for evil spirit beings (Ephesians 6:12).

> *"For we do not wrestle against flesh and blood, but against principalities, against powers, against the rulers of the darkness of this age, against spiritual hosts of wickedness in the heavenly places."*

- Ephesians 6:12

The first location is mentioned as the darkness of this "age," literally in the Greek, "aion" meaning, "World" or "age." The second location mentioned is wickedness in "heavenly" places, referring to the second heaven. The implication is that some evil spirits dwell on this world, while others reside in the second heaven.

We know from scriptures that satan and a third of the angels were cast out of heaven, when they joined in the rebellion against God, however the heaven they were expelled from was the "third heaven," where God dwells. The third heaven is the abode of the triune God. Its location is not revealed (see Matthew 23:34-37; Luke 10:20; and Revelation 22:2, 20-27).

For our purpose, understanding that there are two locations for evil spirits will help in putting into context the war in which we wage.

Angels

In waging an effective fight against the enemy, it is important to understand that satan is an angel. "Angels" are mentioned almost three hundred times in Scripture, and are only absent from books like Ruth, Nehemiah, Esther, the letters of John, and James. Though other words are used for these spiritual beings, the primary word used in the Bible is "angel."

The Hebrew word for angel is "mal`ach," and the Greek word is "angelos." Both words mean "messenger," and describe one who executes the purpose and will of the one whom they serve. The Holy angels are messengers of God, serving Him and doing His bidding. The fallen angels serve satan (the first fallen angel and the god of this world - 2 Corinthians 4:4).

Angels are created beings and not the spirits of departed human beings. From the following scripture, it is clear that Christ not only created the angels, but also their dominion and sphere of influence.

"For by Him all things were created that are in heaven and that are on earth, visible and invisible, whether thrones or dominions or principalities or powers. All things were created through Him and for Him. And He is before all things, and in Him all things consist."

- Colossians 1:16-17

"For by Him (Jesus) all things were created that are in heaven and that are on earth, visible and invisible, whether thrones or dominions or principalities or powers. All things were created through Him and for Him. And He is before all things, and in Him all things consist.

- Colossians 1:16-17

Angels are personal beings and manifest all the features of personhood. In Job 38:7 they are called "the sons of God." They have:

- Self-awareness (Daniel 10:11)
- Self-expression (Acts 12:7-8; Revelation 22:8-9)
- Moral awareness (Matthew 13:41; Luke 15:10)
- Sempiternity or without end (Matthew 25:41)
- Intelligence (2 Samuel 14:20; Revelation 22:16)
- Desire (1 Peter 1:12)
- Emotion (Job 38:7; Revelation 12:12)
- Accountability (1 Corinthians 6:3)

Angels have an angelic nature. Unlike the trichotomous nature of humans (body, soul, and spirit), angels have a spirit nature (Luke 24:37-39; Hebrews 1:1, 7). Their spirit nature is unique and has some form of a celestial body (Daniel 10:5-6; Matthew 28:2-3; Luke 24:4).

Sometimes they have wings, sometime they are like people, and sometimes they are like fire. From the scriptures, it appears that angels are not confined to any specific form or shape, but assume various forms and appearances according to the nature of the work they are required to perform and the will of God. In many instances, they behave and act just as we do. Look at some of the descriptive information in the Bible.

- They sit down (Judges 6:11)
- They stand (Isaiah 6:2)
- They look like women and have wind in their wings (Zechariah 5:9)
- They look like men; and eat (Genesis 18:2, 8)
- They are masculine in gender (Revelation 10:1-3; Matthew 22:30)
- They are like fire (Psalms 104:4)
- They are spirits (Psalms 104:4; Hebrews 1:7)
- They are capable of learning (1 Peter 1:12; Ephesians 3:10)
- They speak and have their own language (1 Corinthians 13:1)
- They play musical instruments (1 Thessalonians 4:16; Revelation 8:2, 6)

We also learn from the Scriptures that they are many (Daniel 7:10; Matthew 26:53; Hebrews 12:22; Revelation 5:11), they are very powerful (Psalms 103:20; 2 Peter 2:11), and they belong to a more superior order in creation than humans. We also know that angels are indestructible. Being created personal creatures with a definite beginning, they will exist forever as either Holy angels with God (Hebrews 12:22-23) or fallen angels bound in hell for all eternity (Matthew 25:41, 46).

Morally, angels are either Holy or evil. They belong to various ranks (Ephesians 1:21; 6:12; Colossians 1:16), with Michael the archangel as the leader of the warring Holy angels (Revelation 12:7-8) and satan as the leader of evil fallen angels (Matthew 25:41). The words "principality" (rule), "power" (authority), "dominion" (lordship), and "might" (power), indicate various angelic positions or spheres of influence and authority in the administrations of both God and satan.

Holy Angels

As stated earlier, angels, whose name means, "messenger," are active in the service of God.

- They render worship (Revelation 5:11-12).
- They deliver messages (Luke 1:11, 26-27).
- They convey divine revelation (Acts 7:53; Revelation 1:1).
- They inflict divine judgments (2 Samuel 24:16-17; Revelation chapters 8-9).
- They influence governments (Daniel 10:12-11:1).
- They deliver dead humans to their destinies (Luke 16:22).
- They care for God's people (Genesis 19:1-22; 1 Kings 19:5-8; Acts 5:19-20; Hebrews 1:14).

- They observe believers (1 Corinthians 4:9; 11:10).
- They war against the forces of satan (Revelation 12:7-9).
- They are assigned to churches (Revelation 2-3)
- They are assigned as guardians to people (Acts 12:13-15; Matthew 18:2-3, 10).

Understanding what Holy angels are and how they interact with Christians, the church, and the enemy, will help us engage an effective battle. Angels are here to assist us in our life mission. When commissioned, they are actively engaged in war against the enemy on our behalf. Angels also often manifest themselves to those operating with the Seer's gift.

Evil Angels

They Scriptures reveal that satan was created Lucifer – "the shining one" (Isaiah 14:12), "the anointed cherib" (Ezekiel 28:13-14), and that he was perfect in all of his ways until he sinned (vs. 15). Having personhood, he had self-determination and the ability to worship. Yet, struck by his own beauty and pride, he chose to exalt himself rather than the Creator (vs. 17). This self-exaltation was a manifestation of the pride in his heart, the first sin (1 Timothy 3:6). Motivated by burning pride, he set out on an irrational course to seize for himself God's authority over the universe (Isaiah 14:12-14). He became the prince of this world when he led man to sin against God and thus transferred man's rule over the earth to himself (Genesis 1:26; 3:1-6; John 12:31; Colossians 1:13; Acts 26:18).

Following the example and leadership of satan, a third of the angelic host revolted with the devil and became members of his kingdom (Revelation 12:4, 7-9; Matthew 12:26; 25:41), severing their original relationship with God. The Scriptures tell us that there are there are two groups of evil angles, the confined fallen angels, and the free fallen angles.

Confined Fallen Angels

To help us understand the confined fallen angels we need to go back in time to the days of Noah.

> *"Now it came to pass, when men began to multiply on the face of the earth, and daughters were born to them, that the sons of God saw the daughters of men, that they were beautiful; and they took wives for themselves of all whom they chose. And the LORD said, "My Spirit shall not strive with man forever, for he is indeed flesh; yet his days shall be one hundred and twenty years." There were giants (Nephilim) on the earth in those days, and also afterward, when the sons of God came in to the daughters of men and they bore children to them. Those were the mighty men who were of old, men of renown.*

> *- Genesis 6:1*

It appears that these "Sons of God" had relations with the "daughters of men" and produced an offspring referred to as giants (Nephilim). It also appears that the women had little to say in the matter. This unnatural union resulted in the procreation of abnormal genetically modified creatures, the

Nephilim, translated giants. Due to this alien invasion these "giants" were designated as the principal reason for the judgment of the Flood. Jude and Peter confirm that the angels involved in this unnatural act were judged by God and cast into hell (Tartarus) until the great Day of Judgment (2 Peter 2:4-8; 1 Peter 3:18-20; Jude 6, 7).

Chuck Missler, noted bible scholar, says this regarding Genesis 6:

> *"The strange events recorded in Genesis 6 were understood by the ancient rabbinical sources, as well as the Septuagint translators, as referring to fallen angels procreating weird hybrid offspring with human women-known as the "Nephilim." So it was also understood by the early church fathers. These bizarre events are also echoed in the legends and myths of every ancient culture upon the earth: the ancient Greeks, the Egyptians, the Hindus, the South Sea Islanders, the American Indians, and virtually all the others."*

- Chuck Missler, "Mischievous Angels or Sethites?"

God's judgment in Genesis 6 was an act of the amazing grace of God. By interceding in this matter He kept the human race intact and uncontaminated by satan's attempts defile Christ's bloodline. If satan had succeeded, Jesus couldn't have been born and the human race would have been lost, forever. By destroying the contaminated race and saving uncontaminated Noah and his immediate uncontaminated family, and by binding the evil fallen angels who participated in this great sin in Hades until the final judgment, God made the way for His plan of Salvation to come about.

From a spiritual warfare standpoint there is no engagement with the confined evil angels, for they are confined, waiting for their final judgment. One thought however, in Revelation 9, John speaks of hearing the sound of a fifth angel, and when it sounded a star fell from heaven to earth, and the key to the bottomless pit was given to him. When he opened the bottomless pit, there arose billows of smoke, and out of the smoke locust like creatures with tails like scorpions, hair like women, teeth like lions, and wings that sounded like mighty horses running into battle, rose and tormented all who were not marked by God. The leader of these creatures was abaddon, in Hebrew, and apollyon, in the Greek. Scholars believe this leader is satan. If so, it is very reasonable to believe that these creatures are the confined evil angels from Genesis chapter six.

Free evil angels

We know, according to Jude, that the confined fallen angels that sinned in Genesis 6 were imprisoned in everlasting chains of darkness. However, the Bible also speaks of a time when another group of evil angels will be kicked out of the heaven (Revelation 12:7-9). Whether this event is historical or yet to occur is not clear. Nor is it clear that this verse is speaking of these angels being kicked out of the third heaven. More than likely, these creatures were kicked out of the third heaven when they rebelled against God, and at some point in the future, when the kingdom of heaven advances towards Christ's second coming, these fallen angels will be kicked out of the second heaven, at which time they will invade earth in full force (Revelation 12:7-9, 12). What is clear is that these fallen evil angels are free today and reside in the second heaven.

Yet, just because God expelled these rebellious angels from heaven, does not mean He clipped their wings, changed their celestial angelic nature, or took their individual created gifting from them. The same is true for unsaved humans or backslidden Christians. No, they are still angels, though evil, through and through. These unconfined or free fallen angels are the same angels Paul refers to in Ephesians 6:

> *"For we do not wrestle against flesh and blood, but against principalities, against powers, against the rulers of the darkness of this age, against spiritual hosts of wickedness in the heavenly places. Therefore take up the whole armor of God, that you may be able to withstand in the evil day, and having done all, to stand."*

> - Ephesians 6:12-13

In this passage, Paul is telling us that there is a powerful evil network of fallen angels residing in the second heaven under the leadership of satan. These fallen angels are organized, powerful, structured, and bent on the destruction of humanity. Earlier we read how Christ created not only the angels, but also their sphere of influence and authority. How we war against fallen angels is different from how we wage war against the demonic.

Jude and Peter make it clear that there is a certain way one should rebuke them, namely speaking in the name and authority of Jesus, through His rebuke, and not speaking of things, we as humans, do not understand. In God's order, they are still dignitaries, though fallen and evil. Consider Jude's comments regarding Michael the archangel's encounter with satan or Peter's comments regarding how angels, who are more powerful than us, deal with the schemes of the enemy.

> *"Likewise also these dreamers defile the flesh, reject authority, and speak evil of dignitaries. Yet Michael the archangel, in contending with the devil, when he disputed about the body of Moses, dared not bring against him a reviling accusation, but said, "The Lord rebuke you!"*

> - Jude 1:8-9

> *"...and especially those who walk according to the flesh in the lust of uncleanness and despise authority. They are presumptuous, self-willed. They are not afraid to speak evil of dignitaries, whereas angels, who are greater in power and might, do not bring a reviling accusation against them before the Lord."*

> - 2 Peter 2:10-11

Jesus himself gave us an example of resisting satan, a fallen angel, by using scripture in Matthew 4 and Luke 4. The power of the Word brings to life the legal truth that satan and his minions are defeated.

Shifting Atmospheres

The most prominent way fallen angels war against us is how they affect the atmosphere of the World.

"And you He made alive, who were dead in tres-
passes and sins, in which you once walked accord-
ing to the course of this world, according to the
prince of the power of the air, the spirit who now
works in the sons of disobedience,"

- Ephesians 2:1-2

Across the second heaven and into our own atmosphere this highly organized enemy force, works to cause the unsaved to follow the ways of this world. The word "air" in this passage refers to the lowest of spiritual heavens. Fallen angels work to create an atmosphere for demons to do their diabolical work. Fallen angels create the right political, social, religious, and philosophical environment that enables demons to influence, and ultimately control, people in their surroundings. There is one word that best describes this atmosphere and that is "culture." Fallen angels create a cultural environment that makes it difficult for people to be saved or for believers to follow Christ with their whole heart.

Where fallen angels have had success, there is a raise in demonic activity. That is why it is essential that we correctly wage an effective warfare against these spiritual forces of evil. Fallen angels at times may do some of the activities of demons. The devil is also called "the tempter" (Matthew 4:3; 1 Thessalonians 3:5), and he is an angel. Therefore, fallen angels can still tempt us. The primary meaning of the word angel is "messenger." A messenger's job is to convey a message or word from another. Fallen angels are very good at feeding people lies in order to carry out their plans.

Unlike demons, fallen angels are not as easily removed from a person, a church, a region, or a nation. Our work to overcome fallen angels requires great effort. Though we may confront them directly in the name of Jesus, we must often employ additional weapons to overcome their effect. Remember, Daniel prayed and fasted for twenty-one days before he saw the "Prince of Persia" (a fallen angel) pushed back from destroying Israel (see Daniel 10:13).

When evil angels are at work in a person, a church, region, or a nation, it will often take more than a simple rebuke to remove them. They are strong beings and will not be easily dislodged from their assignment. In contrast, demons are relatively easy to drive out with a simple order.

Fallen angels are defeated only through intense spiritual warfare. To understand more clearly our strategy for spiritual warfare against fallen angels, we must first recognize who these beings are, what their tactics are, and how they fight. While demons work directly against us, fallen angels use devices that are more indirect in nature. It is easy to recognize demonic attacks. However, what do we do when the spiritual force in heavenly places attack?

Because we are seated with Christ in heavenly realms, we have authority in this realm (Ephesians 2:6), but how we exercise that authority over fallen angels is different from the way we exercise our authority over demons.

Tom Brown, in his book, Devil, Demons, & Spiritual Warfare, outlines seven very practical steps in dealing with fallen angels.

Cast Out Demons – in order to make any progress against the heavenly forces, you must penetrate their strongholds. Casting out demons breaks down satan's frontline. (Luke 10:17-19)

Intercessory Prayer – God directed prayer is agonizing and intense. It is a wrestling prayer in the spirit and is often associated with fasting. Daniel's example is a good case study (Daniel 10:1-4). Paul describes this type of prayer in Galatians 4:19 as pains of childbirth.

Preach the Gospel – Paul says "For I am not ashamed of the gospel of Christ, for it is the power of God to salvation for everyone who believes..." (Romans 1:16). The devils currency is soul. The more souls he has the greater influence he has in the world.

Utilize the Media – Don't wait for the executives in Hollywood to have a change of heart, find ways to use the arts today to shift the cultural messaging in the world. Holy Spirit inspired creativity can influence a community far more than a good sermon from a pulpit (Mark 16:15)

Influence the Schools – Spiritual warfare is more than simply commanding the forces of darkness to leave our nation; it includes engaging the enemy in our schools. We need Spirit filled teachers, administrators, and educators. We need Christians in our libraries, in the PTA, and on the school board.

Get Involved in Politics – Don't believe the lie that Christians aren't supposed to get involved in politics. The terms in Scripture for evil entities are "rulers," "authorities," and "powers." These words come from governmental terms. Even satan is called the "King of Tyre" in Ezekiel 28:12 and the "Prince of Persia in Daniel 10:20. The enemy hates it when true believers get involved in the political process. (See Romans 13:4.)

Obey God – By our obedience we will be ready to punish every act of disobedience (2 Corinthians 10:6). Paul exhorts Timothy that "Moreover he must have a good testimony among those who are outside, lest he fall into reproach and the snare of the devil" (1 Timothy 3:7). Simple acts of obedience will inflict damage on the forces of evil, more than any shouting into the heavens can accomplish.

CHAPTER 10

What are Demons?

*"And these signs will follow those who believe: In
My name they will cast out demons; they will
speak with new tongues; they will take up
serpents; and if they drink anything deadly, it will
by no means hurt them; they will lay hands on
the sick, and they will recover."*

- Mark 17:17-18

*"then the Lord knows how to deliver the godly
out of temptations and to reserve the unjust
under punishment for the day of judgment."*

- 1 Peter 2:9

So we have dealt with the topics of angels, both Holy and evil. Now let's turn our attention to demons. To start with, demons are not the spirits of deceased evil humans. The spirits of deceased evil humans are not free to roam but are confined until judgment (Luke 16:19-31; 2 Peter 2:9). Nor are demons merely personifications of evil, or of natural forces, such as the "gods" of nature, as skeptics assume. Nor are demons the superstitious designation for

particular natural diseases, such as epilepsy or mental illness, because Scripture clearly distinguishes these disorders
from demon possession, although it is possible that both can
be present or that demons can induce mental and physical
illness.

Unlike angels, demons are never described as winged creatures, and they seem to be limited to the earth. Contrary to
popular Christian theory, the fallen angels are not the "demons" of today. The demon inside the madman of Gadara
pleaded with Jesus not to send them out of the area (Mark
5:10). Their only choice was limited to roaming the earth.
They could not fly away into the second heaven. In fact, Jesus
said that when a demon is cast out he wanders through dry
places, seeking rest (Matthew 12:43-45).

demons, on the other hand, are often referred to "wicked,
unclean, evil spirits" and are usually mentioned in relation to
someone who is demonized, and the demon speaks through
that person. demons never appear in a bodily form themselves, but always involve a body of a person or animal they
are working through.

 It is my opinion that demons have their origin in the giants
(Nephilim) who existed before the flood. We know from
Genesis 6 that the entire Nephilim hybrid race died with the
rest of humanity in the Flood except for Noah and his family
(Genesis 6:13, 17, 21-22).

We know that the flood destroyed all life that was upon the
surface of the earth. The Nephilim were also destroyed. If the
fallen angels are being held in chains, they obviously are not
the spirits that enslave so many today. The fallen angels al-

ready have celestial bodies and don't seek any other bodies to inhabit. However, the Nephilim lost their bodies in the Flood, and are constantly seeking bodies to inhabit.

We know that the spirit nature of a person is passed down through the father (study the following: Genesis 2:7; 1 Corinthians 11:8, 12, 15:21-22, 45; Romans 5:12-32; Hebrews 7:9-10; Ezekiel 18:4, 20; James 5:20.) Jesus is a perfect example of this. Since Jesus did not have a literal, biological father, the sin nature was not passed down to Him. However, since He had a human mother, he was fully human but without original sin. Original sin is passed through the soul from the father. Jesus has two natures: God and man. Colossians 2:9 says, "For in Him dwells all the fullness of deity in bodily form." Jesus received His human nature from Mary, but He received His divine nature through God the Holy Spirit. Therefore, Jesus is both God and man. He was sinless, had no original sin, and was both fully God and fully man.

So, in essence, these hybrids had a genetically altered human body and a sinful angelic spirit like their fathers, the evil fallen angels. Now, they wander the earth as tormented disembodied spirits, waiting for their day in judgment where they will join their fallen fathers for all eternity. There is one last scripture I would like to look at regarding the sinful angelic-spirit-nature of demons. In 1 Corinthians Paul makes an obscure reference to angels when discussing the head covering of women in the church.

> *"For this reason the woman ought to have a symbol of authority on her head, because of the angels."*

> - 1 Corinthians 11:10

This reference to angels makes no sense in the context of this passage unless Paul has in the back of his mind the events of Genesis 6. This covering he links to a symbol of authority. The Greek word for authority in this passage is "exousia" meaning "power," "one who possesses authority," or "wears a crown." Many commentators brush over this verse, not knowing how to deal with Paul's statement. However, it is my opinion that Paul, in the context of Genesis 6, is reminding the angelic community that women in the church, these female children of God, are endued with power and authority from the Most High God, are covered by Him, and are princesses in the Kingdom of God. They are not to be looked at in an unholy manor. As well as reminding women in the church of their Holy position and authority in the Kingdom of God.

demons and Necromancy

Necromancy is the sin that entrapped my family for so long. God forbade the Israelites to be involved with various types of magic, familiar spirits, and necromancy (Leviticus 20:27).

According to the Strong's, the word for "familiar spirit" means "ghost, spirit of a dead one, necromancy, one who evokes a dead one, one with a familiar spirit". If one considers that demons are actually the spirits of the dead giants (Nephilim), then it makes sense then that demons are being referenced to as "ghost, spirit of a dead one." Moreover, it is forbidden for God's people to "evoke the spirit of a dead one", or to have anything to do with a demon, let alone to become familiar, gain familiarity, with one. The term for "medium" is "one who has a familiar spirit" and "necromancer," again this is having a relationship with a demon.

> *"When you come into the land which the LORD your God is giving you, you shall not learn to follow the abominations of those nations. There shall not be found among you anyone who makes his son or his daughter pass through the fire, or one who practices witchcraft, or a soothsayer, or one who interprets omens, or a sorcerer, or one who conjures spells, or a medium, or a spiritist, or one who calls up the dead. For all who do these things are an abomination to the LORD, and because of these abominations the LORD your God drives them out from before you."*

- Deuteronomy 18:9-12

Some of these same terms are used again in Deuteronomy 18, forbidding the people to practice or to consult with anyone who practiced, having a relationship with a demon. God calls this an abomination, and makes clear that those nations around at the time all did practice these things. Thank God for His amazing grace that He intervened in my family and in my life!

CHAPTER 11

Revelatory Insight

"...to another faith by the same Spirit, to another gifts of healings by the same Spirit, to another the working of miracles, to another prophecy, to another discerning of spirits, to another different kinds of tongues, to another the interpretation of tongues.....:

- 1 Corinthians 12:9-10

"But the manifestation of the Spirit is given to each one for the profit of all: for to one is given the word of wisdom through the Spirit, to another the word of knowledge through the same Spirit, to another faith by the same Spirit, to another gifts of healings by the same Spirit, to another the working of miracles, to another prophecy, to another discerning of spirits, to another different kinds of tongues, to another the interpretation of tongues. But one and the same Spirit works all these things, distributing to each one individually as He wills"

- 1 Corinthians 12:7-11

For the Seer, the gifts of the "words of knowledge" and the "discerning of spirits" usually come through the lens of visions and dreams, though visions are the most common. Visions and even dreams can also play a role in your personal preparation and study of effective spiritual warfare. I have classified the following areas as it relates to the Seer's gift and warfare.

Instructional Visions and Dreams: These often occur when the Holy Spirit is guiding you into further study on spiritual warfare. When I first became a Christian, I didn't have a clue as to what was biblical and what was demonic. All I knew was that Jesus loved me. During my first year as a Christian, they Lord would often give me dreams and visions relating to spiritual warfare. All of which, lead me into an in depth study of the scriptures as it related not only to warfare, but Christian apologetics as a whole. Many of the lessons the Lord showed me started in seed form, as He spoke to me in dreams and showed me in visions. Through the prompting of the Holy Spirit and teaching from great mentors, I not only built a strong biblical foundation for my faith, but was awakened to the truth that the spiritism that I grew up with was in fact, inspired by the demons. This newfound awareness led me in preparation and prayer for freedom of my whole family.

Discerning of Spirits and satanic Generational Assignments: Often the Lord will use visions or dreams to give insight revealing the satanic forces operating in an individual's life and/or family. This can be connected to a curse, the sins of the fathers, or directly related to a door being opened to the occult.

One such event I would like to share involved my family's deliverance from satan's grasp. For the first eighteen months of being a Christian, the Lord would not allow me to confront my family regarding Spiritism and the occult. The night He did release me was indeed an amazing night.

My family had been a burden on my heart for some time. During this season in my life, the Lord had been immersing me in the things of the Spirit. I felt like I was in spiritual boot camp and Jesus was my drill sergeant. The Lord had put me on fast track and was teaching a great deal regarding the scriptures and power of the Holy Spirit in my life. Then one night the Lord showed me the satanic forces that were commissioned to destroy my family and me.

That night I awakened full of the Holy Spirit and praying in tongues. As I sat up, I turned to look at my wife. She was sitting up in bed and her head was shaking violently side-to-side. As I prayed, she slowly stopped and lay back down, continuing her sleep. During this event, she was asleep and to this day, she does not remember the event. As she lay down, I looked beyond her to the door of our bedroom. The presence of the Holy Spirit began to magnify all over me.

Standing in the doorway, I saw, what I understood was a fallen angel dressed in ancient warrior attire. I knew in my spirit that this was the enemy. Next to him was a demon spirit. Instantly, I was aware that this was a high-ranking evil angel and he had authority over the smaller demonic minion. The fallen angel was unable to enter the room. However, he stood his ground for several minutes and appeared to be confident. I also knew that the smaller demon was weaker in power and authority for he could not even look into the room. As I prayed, I felt the presence of the Lord intensify, then suddenly, they both disappeared.

They had come to mess with my family and do harm to my wife. This started my quest towards intersession for my family. As I pondered this event, I felt that they were somehow tied to my background in the occult and were trying to destroy my newly found life in Christ. I was not sure if the Lord had given me an open vision or if He simply opened my eyes to see what was happening in the spirit realm.

A week went by with heavy intersession and study. Then one night the Lord gave me a dream. In this dream, I saw my Aunt's house. I was looking at the back patio door from above. As I watched, I saw my uncle Bill and Aunt Eva arrive home. Suddenly, I saw dozens of spirits flying above them as they entered the house. Then the same creature that was in my house was hovering over them. Then I woke, praying.

Instantly, all the dots began to connect, and I understood that this was the principality assigned to my family for generations. As I prayed, I asked the Lord if I could go down to San Diego and pray for my family. He said, "It's not time." Then, about a week later, while I was worshiping, the Lord spoke to me and said, "It's time."

I instantly called my father and told him I had to meet with the family. When I arrived at my Aunt's house in San Diego, to my surprise, my father had called all his brothers and sisters to come over and listen to what I had to say. I walked into the house, filled with the Holy Spirit. I was greeted with a loving warm welcome and proceeded to the living room where I found all my Aunts and Uncles sitting there waiting for me.

I sat there and began to share my testimony, how Jesus came and set me free. My Aunt knew about the dream the Lord had given me, how He spoke to me two years earlier (see chapter 23 about my story), because I ran to her to find out what the dream meant. At that time, we had a séance and the table went crazy. It actually kicked a bible off the table. That was the last time I had seen my Aunt, up until this moment. Now with newly worn Bible in hand I shared with them the truth of God's Word and the reality of the demonic world.

As I was sharing, I could see the Holy Spirit speaking into their lives. I looked over at my Uncle Paul and he and Aunt Gladis had a big smile on their faces. My Uncle Paul chimed in:

> *"Fred, I know what you're talking about. The spirit activity got so bad in our house that we could not even sleep at night. The furniture would move and the bed would shake. We were scared to death. Then we saw Oral Roberts on TV and he was coming to San Diego. We knew we had to do something so we down to the coliseum and went forward to get prayer. Your aunt and I were saved and healed that night. All of the demonic attacks that happened to us stopped instantly and have never come back. I don't know why we didn't tell anybody. But it's the God's honest truth."*

I was blown away; I knew I wasn't alone in this. After they shared their testimony, I walked my Aunt Eva through the scriptures and shared with them everything relating to the occult. I asked them if they would mind if I pray for them. They all eagerly said yes. As I prayed, I could feel God's presence fill the house. However, I still was not sure of my Aunt Eva's stance on all this.

Later that night, my Aunt Eva was washing dishes in the kitchen. Then I heard her call my name in a sad and weakened voice. When I walked into the kitchen she had her head down on the sink. "Aunt Eva, are you ok?"

The she said, "Fred, please pray for me, and she collapsed to the kitchen floor."

I grabbed her hand and caressed her. Then I began to pray. As I prayed, I spoke to the demons and commanded them to leave her in the name of Jesus. My dear Aunt began to cry even more. I held her and walked her through the steps of salvation. My sweet Aunt went down in tears, came up free, and saved as a child of the King. Together we prayed through renunciation and I shared with her the power of the Holy Spirit and the assurance of salvation. That night started a ripple effect in my Dad's side of the family and all of them came to the Lord. Moreover, my Aunt Eva became my closest confidant in things of the spirit.

You see, my family had opened the door to the occult and for close to a hundred years we were generationally bound to powers in the heavenly realm. All the while God was working behind the scenes to end the power this stronghold had over our family. I am convinced that the hardest part of the battle happened during that year of intersession. I am also convinced that during that time God had commissioned His angelic team to intercede on our behalf and bind the fallen angels and demonic forces assigned to our family.

Discerning of Spirits in General: The Discerning of Spirits is a Supernatural revelation from the Spirit of God, which opens one's eyes to the activities of the spirit realm. The event described earlier is a perfect example of this activity. Through the operation of this Gift one can see Jesus, the Holy Spirit, the similitude of God, Angels, satan, demons and any other spirit beings, objects or spiritual activities. This Gift also enables the possessor to discern the power, good or evil, which prompts certain behaviors in other living beings. (Numbers 22:27-35; Mark 8:33; John 1:47; 6:70)

Anytime an individual experiences a Holy Spirit induced inward vision, open vision, trance, or dream in which the Spirit realm is looked into, the Discerning of Spirits is in operation.

I have experienced the Discerning of Spirits frequently operating with the other Revelatory Gifts on many occasions. I have had visitations of Jesus and Angels through open visions, a trance and dreams. I have been called to intersession by the Lord via dreams and trances where He shared with me the strategies of the enemy in given situation. I have seen the Holy Spirit give insight into the root cause of a man under demon oppression. I have seen open visions of a demonic stronghold over the face of an individual. I have seen in the spirit a demon on the back of an individual.

The Discerning of Spirits is a tremendous Gift indeed and a very powerful gift in dealing with the demonic. Through its operation, come protection, direction, correction, connection, revelation, emancipation and provision.

Words of Knowledge in General: The Word of Knowledge is a Supernatural revelation from the mind of God. It is unrelated to natural, human knowledge. It always has to do with people, places, events, or things. It always, and only, deals with the past or the present. It never has to do with future events. Things revealed in the future fall under the gift of Prophecy. Let's look at an example of the Word of Knowledge from Jesus' Ministry. Jesus met a woman at a well one day. He wanted to prove to her who He was so He challenged her.

> *"Jesus said to her, "Go, call your husband, and come here." The woman answered and said, "I have no husband." Jesus said to her, "You have well said, 'I have no husband,' for you have had five husbands, and the one whom you now have is not your husband; in that you spoke truly." The woman said to Him, "Sir, I perceive that You are a prophet."*

> - John 4:16-19

Here Jesus supernaturally revealed part of this woman's past. He told her that she had been married five times. Then Jesus revealed something about her present life. He told her that she was presently shacking up with a man she hadn't even bothered to marry! The woman realized that she was encountering supernatural revelation knowledge.

This is an excellent example of the Word of Knowledge. It has to do with people and events. It also has to do with both the past and the present. Notice something else in this narrative. Jesus only revealed certain parts of this woman's life. He didn't reveal everything about her life. That's why it's called a "Word" of Knowledge. A word is a fragmentary part of a sentence. A Word of Knowledge is only a fragmentary part of all that God knows.

Let me share one example of the Word of Knowledge, as it relates to deliverance.

Several years ago an associate of mine, whom I will call Steve, went off to Bible College in central Florida. I hadn't seen him for several months until one day Steve came by to see me at the restaurant. We got to talk and I could sense that he was troubled and really needed some counsel. I asked Steve if he would like to go for a walk and pray. He said, "yes," so we headed down to the parking garage below the restaurant.

I asked Steve what was going on and he became very erratic. He started crying. I could see shame and fear over his countenance. I asked him what was going on and all he could say was, "I can't think. I can't stop it. I don't know what's wrong with me. I try, and try, and try, nothing seems to help."

I started praying for him and as I was praying I saw a picture of Steve crouched on his knees with his head down chained to a wall. I asked the Lord what this was, and instantly I understood that he was bound to a demonic stronghold. I shared this picture with him, and said that I think he was bound to a lie from the enemy. When I said that, he immediately started weeping. He kept saying in a voice of anguish, "Make it go away." Then he fell to the ground and started shaking violently. All the while I was praying, asking the Lord for more information. At that moment, I felt that his situation was had to do with his sexual identity. I placed my hand on his shoulder and spoke to his spirit to be at peace. He started to relax.

Then I said, "Steve, are you having difficulty in the area of sexuality?"

He started to cry, even more. I told him that I believed that the enemy was binding him to a lie and that Jesus was going to set him free. I told him that Jesus had created him wholly as a man and that the enemy was feeding him lies and driving him to this unnatural lust. He sneered at me. Then I spoke to the evil spirit and commanded it to be silent. Steve just looked up at me with sadness and fear in his eyes. I said, "Steve, do you believe that Jesus is here and that He has come to set you free?"

"Yes," he cried.

Then I spoke to the spirit and said, "You lying spirit of lust, I command you to leave, in the name of Jesus." Steve started to get sick. "You have no authority to punish this man of God." I told the demon, "Jesus said, 'you will know the truth, and the truth will make you free'," and his head perked up. Then I spoke to the demon and said, "I cancel your lies over this brother's mind and command you to leave, now." At that, Steve began to shake and throw-up in the garage. At that moment, the peace of God came over him. I knew that Steve was free. I asked Steve how he felt. He told me it was gone. He explained what was happening to him and how, when he was younger he struggled with his manhood. He had fought this on and off most of his life, but when he started going to Bible School, the struggle intensified.

Steve's situation is like so many that are held captive to the lies of the enemy. And when we believe the lies we give the enemy permission to punish us because we think the lies are true. Captives are people that have been captured in battle and held as POWs. Only the truth will release the stronghold of the enemy. It is important to understand how people get bound in order to be effective in setting them free. In Isaiah 61:1 it says:

> "The Spirit of the Lord GOD is upon Me, Because the LORD has anointed Me To preach good tidings to the poor; He has sent Me to heal the brokenhearted, To proclaim liberty to the captives, And the opening of the prison to those who are bound;"

There are two types of people bound in this passage. The first are captives, and the second are prisoners. A captive is taken and imprisoned through lies and deception. A prisoner is a criminal whom a judge sentences to jail. It takes the knowledge of Truth to set a captive free. Prisoners, on the other hand our bound by their own actions.

In Matthew 18:21-35, Jesus talks about forgiveness, and how it relates to being a prisoner.

> "Then Peter came to Him and said, "Lord, how often shall my brother sin against me, and I forgive him? Up to seven times?"
>
> Jesus said to him, "I do not say to you, up to seven times, but up to seventy times seven. Therefore the kingdom of heaven is like a certain king who wanted to settle accounts with his servants. And when he had begun to settle

accounts, one was brought to him who owed
him ten thousand talents. But as he was not
able to pay, his master commanded that he be
sold, with his wife and children and all that he
had, and that payment be made.

The servant therefore fell down before him,
saying, 'Master, have patience with me, and I
will pay you all.' Then the master of that servant was moved with compassion, released
him, and forgave him the debt.

"But that servant went out and found one of
his fellow servants who owed him a hundred
denarii; and he laid hands on him and took
him by the throat, saying, 'Pay me what you
owe!' So his fellow servant fell down at his feet
and begged him, saying, 'Have patience with
me, and I will pay you all.' And he would not,
but went and threw him into prison till he
should pay the debt.

So when his fellow servants saw what had
been done, they were very grieved, and came
and told their master all that had been done.

Then his master, after he had called him, said
to him, 'You wicked servant! I forgave you all
that debt because you begged me. Should you
not also have had compassion on your fellow
servant, just as I had pity on you?'

And his master was angry, and delivered him
to the torturers until he should pay all that
was due to him. "So My heavenly Father also
will do to you if each of you, from his heart,
does not forgive his brother his trespasses."

It is clear, from the story that un-forgiveness can lead to demonic torment. It opens the door and gives the demonic legal permission to oppress and torture you. Freedom comes from the decree of the King, which in turn give us the authority to command these evil spirits to leave. Without walking a prisoner through the steps of forgiveness, any release from the demonic will only be temporal. It takes the power of the Holy Spirit to get free and stay free of demonic oppression.

The Word of Knowledge in the example I shared help distinguish why Steve was bound. The Word of Knowledge is very powerful. It brings fear and repentance to sinners and blessings to God's people. Most of all, it brings great glory to God.

When you receive a Word of Knowledge, it is important for the Seer to get a clear interpretation from the Lord and understand it application. God gives words of knowledge in several ways:

- Seeing, as in visions and dreams
- Feeling, as in a sharp pain or sensation
- Reading, as in you see words written in your mind
- An Impression, as in thinking or sensing a condition
- Speaking, as in while you are speaking to someone unpremeditated words tumble out of your mouth
- Experience it, as in having a vivid trance or 3D vision, beyond a simple picture

Remember Words of Knowledge can come very fast or be vague. Often the tendency it to brush it off as nothing, learn to focus and tune into what the Holy Spirit is saying. Don't be presumptuous, be humble. Be as specific as you can but don't elaborate. Moreover, most of all don't be afraid. Don't let fear rob you and the person who might have been delivered. Faith is a verb, you have to step out. God gives you information because He wants to use you to set people free.

Visions to the One Being Set Free: Sometimes the Lord will use visionary language to nudge a captive in order to move them to a position to be set free. When this happens, it is a beautiful sovereign move by God to display His tenderness and love. To illustrate this let me share one story.

Thanksgiving week, 2004 I got a surprise knock on the door. When I opened it, it was my son Jamisen asking if he could stay with us. I was so excited; I turned our living room into a bedroom and got him a job in the kitchen at our resort. Jamisen broke-up with his girlfriend and was devastated. He said, "Dad, I need to come back to the Lord – would you pray with me." We walked down to the dock, below our house. I told him the story of the prodigal, how the father loved his son so much that he leaped off his porch and came running to his son while he was still far off. He put rings on his fingers, shoes on his feet, and a robe on his back – then he threw him a killer party, fatted calf and all. We sat, cried, and prayed together. I had gotten my son back. What I didn't know was in just a few short months, on January 19, 2005, he would be killed.

The great sadness entered in my life. My boy was gone. He was accidently struck in the back of the head by a bullet. The following months, to help in my grief, I wrote a book called "Reflections from the Kitchen, a look at Christ through the Eyes of a Chef." The folks in my kitchen helped Jan and I walk through our grief. However, the sadness never really goes away.

We didn't have a church in that area. It was very rural. Then a funny thing began to happen. The girls in the kitchen kept coming to my office for prayer. Usually it was for healing or for mending relationship – and you know what? God started answering their prayers. People were being healed. Most of my culinary team was Spanish and my Spanish is what you call "kitchen Spanish." What started with two Marias and Rosa soon became 20 people, praying daily in the employee cafeteria.

This thing was getting big. By now, my cooks were bringing family members to my office. "Con usted permiso jefe, mi moma..." I would look over and see a little old Spanish lady standing there who needed prayer because she couldn't walk well... And God healed her.

I said, "God this is crazy, what should I do?" So I started "Cooks for Christ" and began having weekly meetings in our banquet room. I bought cases of Spanish/English bibles and began handing them out. By Christmas of that year, at our first 2006 Cooks for Christmas Party, we had 150 people, families, kids, teenagers, grandparents.

One such teenager was Juana's daughter – Juana used to be called Maria. However, her husband had brutally raped her daughter and they had to go into hiding. She disappeared for a year, returned to Mexico, and came back as Juana. Juana had walked into my office, crying. Rosa interpreted her broken English. She told me what had happened, and that something was wrong with her daughter. She would black out –

our just pass out. She asked me to come to their house and pray for them.

When I arrived at Juana's house, her son explained how someone was trying to put a curse on them painting sanetra symbols on their walls in blood. Salendra (not her real name), her daughter had just got home. Juana called her over. "Salendra, this is my chef, he is going to pray for you." We hugged and I asked her to sit down.

When I started to pray for her – she blacked out like a rag doll right in front of me. I thought I was going over for some inner healing or something. I had to pray and get some insight from Poppa. I asked the oldest boy to show me the symbols on the wall. He walked me down the hall to the bedroom and showed me the symbols on the outside wall. What I was really doing was praying in my prayer language and looking for a word from Poppa. I turned to look at Salendra down the hallway and her head suddenly popped up – she was staring at me with her head turned.

"Thank you Poppa." I knew what I was dealing with when I saw the demon's fear in her eyes. I turned and walked back. Immediately, I started to pray, and command this demon to leave her. She started to pass out again. I commanded the demon to release her and loose her mind. She snapped to attention, and after about 15 minutes of back and forth – it was gone. She started to glow. I wanted to make sure it was gone.

She kept saying, "I am free, I am free." Then she said, "It left when I saw you standing before the throne of God singing...

and it left." She said when she saw that vision she knew that God loved her and that she knew I was a servant of His.

I knew at that moment that she was indeed free. I led her to Christ in His fullness, and walked her through forgiveness, and she was filled with the Holy Spirit. The demon that had driven her abuser to brutalize her had come upon her, and the Lord, in a way that only He can do, set this child free.

Well at this Christmas party, she had brought ten of her high school friends with her, folks that knew her and witnessed what Jesus had done. Like the woman at the well, she could not contain herself and shared her freedom to all her friends.

CHAPTER 12

Dealing with demons

"Then the seventy returned with joy, saying, "Lord, even the demons are subject to us in Your name." And He said to them, "I saw Satan fall like lightning from heaven. Behold, I give you the authority to trample on serpents and scorpions, and over all the power of the enemy, and nothing shall by any means hurt you. Nevertheless do not rejoice in this, that the spirits are subject to you, but rather rejoice because your names are written in heaven."

- Luke 10:17-20

"Then the seventy returned with joy, saying, "Lord, even the demons are subject to us in Your name."
And He said to them, "I saw Satan fall like lightning from heaven. Behold, I give you the authority to trample on serpents and scorpions, and over all the power of the enemy, and nothing shall by any means hurt you. Nevertheless do not rejoice in this, that the spirits are subject to you,

*but rather rejoice because your names are
written in heaven."*

- Luke 10:17-20

Although satan and his minions are defeated and will ultimately be cast into the lake of fire, the devil is still very active in his warfare against humanity. It is therefore critical that Christians prepare themselves for the battles that is ahead. We do this by:

Be not ignorant of his devices (2 Corinthians 2:11). The enemy takes advantage of our spiritual immaturity and ignorance (Ephesians 4:11-15).

Constantly strengthen ourselves in the Lord (Ephesians 6:10). When we daily feed on the Scriptures and walk in fellowship with the Lord, then we can meet the enemy in the Lord's strength.

Put on the whole armor of God (Ephesians 6:11-18). The armor of God consists of spiritual realities which we are able to appropriate to our daily lives. These realities are spiritual qualities found in Christ and that manifest Him in our lives. Jesus is the complete armor, He lacks nothing. Let us consider each piece of the armor of God:

Gird your waste with the belt of truth (Ephesians 6:14; John 14:6). The truth here is twofold. First it is the truth of the Word of God and the nature of Jesus Christ. Secondly, the truth is your personal character that you walk in truthfulness and honesty in your daily life. The belt holds up our pants, enabling us to walk in truth and not be hindered or uncovered.

Putting on the breastplate of righteousness (Ephesians 6:14; Philippians 1:11). The breastplate shields the vital organs. Knowing that you have Christ's righteousness (Romans 5:1; 1 Corinthians 1:30) enables you to walk from a kingdom perspective. It is also a call to walk a righteous life.

Wearing the sandals of the preparation of the gospel of peace (Ephesians 6:15; 2 Corinthians 5:20). This refers to our willingness to serve and bear witness to the lost (Acts 16:30-31). This is about motivation of the heart (Romans 1:14-16).

Take up the shield of faith (Ephesians 6:16; Galatians 2:20). Without faith, it is impossible to please God. The Lord wants us to trust Him with all our hearts and believe in all the promises of God. Faith in God, that He is good all the time and He has given us all things in Christ Jesus, will quench the flaming arrows of the evil one.

Put on the helmet of salvation (Ephesians 6:17; Hebrews 13:6). This represents the essential knowledge of salvation and the experience of its deliverance in our daily lives. We need to walk in the assurance of our salvation.

The sword of the Spirit (Ephesians 6:17; John 1:14). This is the Word of God, wielded in the power of the Holy Spirit. To use the Word of God we must learn its content, obey its commands, and depend upon the Holy Spirit to help us to apply it to the various needs of life.

Maintain communication and fellowship with God (Ephesians 6:18a). God is a God of relationship. He desires daily fellowship with Him. We do this through worship, prayer, and reading Scripture.

Be alert for the enemy (Ephesians 6:18b). "Be sober, be vigilant; because your adversary the devil walks about like a roaring lion, seeking whom he may devour"(1 Peter 5:8). He is looking for those who have lost sight of their Lord and have relied upon their own strength in this life. He is looking for chinks in your armor that he can exploit. Our call is to be alert.

Deliverance

"Deliverance" is setting a person free from the oppression of a demonic spirit. demons seek to harass people and, if possible, to move into them. They are restless if they cannot move into a human being. (See Matthew 12:43-45.) When given the opportunity, a demonic spirit will torment or manipulate the host in various ways. Understanding demonic spirits and deliverance is of great importance to the church, because of the adverse effect such spirits can have on believers, on church unity, and on evangelism.

I will use the term "oppression" rather than the term "possession" in the remainder of this chapter, because possession implies ownership and complete control. Since, the Lord Jesus Christ has purchased a believer, he cannot be possessed by the demonic. However, many believers have been host to the demonic prior to conversion, and these evil spirits do not always leave when the host is converted. That is why it is so very important to have in your arsenal the tools for deliverance during times of evangelism. demonic oppression is an enemy of evangelizing, as it prevents the Christian from achieving victory over certain sins, habits, or problems, and thus impairs his testimony as to the power of Jesus to change lives.

Philip is a good model for evangelistic encounters.

> *"Therefore those who were scattered went everywhere preaching the word. Then Philip went down to the city of Samaria and preached Christ to them. And the multitudes with one accord heeded the things spoken by Philip, hearing and seeing the miracles which he did. For unclean spirits, crying with a loud voice, came out of many who were possessed; and many who were paralyzed and lame were healed. And there was great joy in that city."*

- Acts 8:5-8

Phillip was a gifted evangelist. The signs that accompanied his ministry included miracles, healing, and deliverance. I think the church has often missed this formula for evangelism. The ideal time to set free the demonized lost is during the evangelistic process. By not doing so we end up saving those bound by the demonic, and have not positioned them to be free of their tormentors. First, we should cast out their demons, secondly, we should baptize them in the name of Jesus Christ, and lastly, we should lay hands on them and fill them with the Holy Spirit. Only then will they be able to begin their walk with Christ, unhindered by the baggage they used to carry.

The effect of demonic oppression

A demon may torment the host person with such problems as nightmares, unreasonable fear, general accusations of worthlessness or guilt, shame, pain, depression, irrational behavior, and the like. They can give the host an unwelcome and sometimes apparently uncontrollable desire to sin in a particular way, such as a spirit of adultery, or of pornography, or of anger, or of addiction, as examples.

A demon can push the host person repeatedly into sins and habits he resists and wishes to be free from, and thus be a major cause of disaffection and backsliding. After repeated cycles of committing a particular sin the believer may become discouraged and leave the church, or he may live a life of quiet desperation in the church, not realizing he can be free from such oppression.

demonic spirits sometimes cause disease, and sometimes impede or prevent healing of injuries and disease. Jesus cast out spirits of deafness, dumbness, and epilepsy among others.

demons can carry a weight of spiritual and emotional oppression, which dulls spiritual perception and can cause depression. In Isaiah 61:3, it is referred to as "the spirit of heaviness."

A demon may work steadily in a host person, or it may remain quiet, perhaps for years, and then work strongly in him at a later time, perhaps after the host person has achieved a position of spiritual responsibility and status.

The remedy for demonic oppression is deliverance. Deliverance has always been a sign to unbelievers of the power of God over satan.

Personal Preparation and the Deliverance Process

Below is a list of a few key things to remember when dealing with the demonic.

Love: Behind every deliverance is the heart of God's love for the victim. Seek to be a channel for His love and always minister in God's love.

Order: Demons understand and respect authority. If you are ministering in a team environment, make sure there are clear lines of responsibility. Evil spirits will feed off any dissention or confusion in the ranks.

Understand the Limitations: It is useless to expel a demon against the oppressed person's will. If someone is unwilling to change their lifestyle that caused the mess to begin with and that person is unwilling to renounce their agreement with the enemy, specifically and audibly, if you cast it out, it will return and possibly bring others with it. (See Matthew 12:43-45)

Access: Remember that a demon cannot oppress a person unless some avenue of access has been opened to it; such as unforgiveness, hate, abuse, sin, unclean sex, trauma, or some other circumstance.

Legalistic: Demons are very legalistic, typically refusing to leave a person unless their avenues of entrance are renounced by the host person. The objective is to 1.) to expel and 2.) to close all avenues of access to prevent them from returning.

Flexibility: Remember that the prayee is a hurting person and may have been bound for years. Be ready and open to change gears and focus on the healing of wounds or illness.

Teams: Always work in a team of at least two, and never minister to the opposite sex alone. If there is a need to touch the person, make sure only one person does it.

Priority: Make sure that the victim gets your full attention. Be loving but firm. Be encouraging so the prayee sees hope. Let the victim know that Jesus can set them free. Remember, they may have lost all hope.

Silence: If the spirit is manifesting make it be quiet and submit to you in the name of Jesus.

The Prayee: Establish and maintain communication with the prayee. Don't start to minister until you are in the right frame of mind and you have established communication. Do not speak out or pray loudly. Touching and speaking loudly tends to keep the spirit stirred up. You need the spirit quiet so you can talk to the prayee. Above all, be calm.

Authority: If the prayee gets up and starts to move around, take authority over the spirit out loud, and tell the prayee to come and sit down. If the spirit of the prayee speaks, growls, threatens, argues with you, or gives you orders and ask questions, do not speak to it except to order it to be quiet, in the name of Jesus, and take your legal control.

Freedom: Make sure you ask the prayee if he wants to be free from the situation and try to make sure he actually wants to get free.

Jesus: Make sure the prayee has accepted Jesus as his Savior and Lord.

Interview: Interview the prayee to discover the event or events, or relationship situations, that have led to the bondage.

Closing Doors: Lead the prayee in closing all open doors that have given access to the demonic.

Forgiveness: Lead the prayee to forgive the one that hurt them or led them to wrong conduct.

Repentance: Lead the prayee through repentance of each of the prayee's own sins in the situation, and specifically asking for God's forgiveness.

Renounce: Lead the prayee to renounce all the spirits involved, in the name of Jesus.

Bondage: Break the bondage that caused the sin, the conduct, the attitude, the spirit, the vow, or the curse, as indicated, in the name of Jesus.

Cast Out: Cast out the demon or demons in the name of Jesus.

Finish: When you think you have finished, ask the Holy Spirit if there is additional issues that need to be dealt with. If so, cast them out.

Praise: Ask the prayee to praise and thank Jesus for his deliverance.

In Filling: Ask the prayee to pray for the Holy Spirit to fill him, and to fill all the places formerly occupied by evil spirits.

CHAPTER 13

My Story

"Nebuchadnezzar the king, 'To all peoples, nations, and languages that dwell in all the earth: Peace be multiplied to you. I thought it good to declare the signs and wonders that the Most High God has worked for me. How great are His signs, and how mighty His wonders! His kingdom is an everlasting kingdom, and His dominion is from generation to generation....

And at the end of the time I, Nebuchadnezzar, lifted my eyes to heaven, and my understanding returned to me; and I blessed the Most High and praised and honored Him who lives forever: For His dominion is an everlasting dominion, and His kingdom is from generation to generation.

All the inhabitants of the earth are reputed as nothing; He does according to His will in the army of heaven and among the inhabitants of the earth. No one can restrain His hand or say to Him, "What have You done?" ...

Now I, Nebuchadnezzar, praise and extol and honor the King of heaven, all of whose works

are truth, and His ways justice. And those who
walk in pride He is able to put down."

- Daniel 4:1-3, 34-37

The testimony of Jesus is the Spirit of prophecy. This is my testimony, how I came to know Jesus and my walk with Him in the world of the prophetic. Nebuchadnezzar, after encountering God through dreams and the ministry of Daniel, had this to say.

You see, there comes a time in everyone's life, of deep reflection, a time of looking at all the hidden things in your life and assessing where you stand in relationship with the living God. This is a powerful and beautiful experience. Yet, more often than not, it's a two-sided coin.

My own journey into the realm of prophetic dreams and visions didn't come about by a Christian desiring a spiritual gift, though Paul admonishes us to do that. Nor did it come about by being a disciple by the gifted hand of a seasoned prophet in the school of the prophets, yet I would recommend this highly. My journey is more comparable a seed trying to burst through the soil of life. This story is a glimpse through the windows of my heart. How God entered into an impossible situation and replaced the dungeon doors of my life with stained glass windows. Windows that now, with the light of His glory, radiates the splendor of the one who died for my sins.

The story begins, not with me, but with my grandfather, Ernest Asa Raynaud. In a time in history when the world was in a state of confusion and dissolution, World War I had ended. Germany's war efforts were collapsed. Woodrow Wilson had announced his fourteen points for peace, while Charlie Chaplin was bringing laughter to the hearts of many, with his new movie, "Shoulder Arms."

At that time, Grandpa, a stout man with broad shoulders and an iron grip that sent a blow to the handshake of all that greeted him, was working his way through the ring, as a boxer. He had met my grandmother, Alice Mary Lowell, daughter of Adelbert Lowell, who served as a Captain in the US Navy during the Civil War. The Lowell's were an old American family, with ancestors as James Russell Lowell, famous American poet and Statesman, and France Cabot Lowell, who started the first water-powered textile mill in this country, and founded the city of Lowell, Massachusetts.

Grandma's family was aristocratic, but in 1898, when the Spanish-American war erupted, Grandma or Nana as I called her, was sent to a convent in Santa Rosa, California, where she would spend much of her childhood. At the age of seventeen, she moved to San Francisco. It was not long after the great earthquake of 1906 that Grandpa and Nana came together. Both had been survivors of the great quake and, up to the time of her death in 1978, she still received annual letters from the White House honoring her as one of a few survivors.

Gramps had an unshakable love for this woman. She was a petite lady, with gentleness about her. She was a butterfly, timid and meek, and at the same time, afraid and startled at the slightest unexpected move. I think it was this quality that attracted Grandpa, it was different from the rugged way he lived his life.

In 1910, they moved to San Diego, California. They rented a small Spanish style home with a tiny yard. It had a pot-bellied stove and an icebox to store all the perishables. It was an active neighborhood. Often you would see the ice cream man or vegetable man come by in a horse drawn cart. Grandpa's favorite caller was a short black lady, dressed in a white dress and white turban. She would push her cart up the street three times a week, selling hot hominy.

The year the First World War ended my father was born (also known as the Great War). They named him Liberty Earnest Raynaud, third in a family of three boys and one girl. They all grew up during the great depression, yet they did not seem to know it or feel the pain of it. San Diego was different then, and for a kid, life was an adventure. Streetcars would take you to the beach where you could camp or go smelt fishing with a bamboo pole. Now and then, they would take a trip to Young's Cave or hop a freight train and eat dinner at the hobo jungles next to the railroad tracks. The train rides were beautiful; nature came alive with wild flowers, sour-grass, and California poppies everywhere.

It is hard for me to imagine life back then, without all the pollution, noise, and people running around with no place to go. Yet, life was no picnic either, not even close. People were trying to come together, to get back what they had lost during the war where nine million people had lost their lives. All of a sudden, it happened... the great influenza epidemic hit... and people were powerless, standing by while young and old struggled to survive.

In one year, 1918-1919, when the pandemic hit twenty five million people had died around the world and estimated 850,000 men, women, and children died in the U.S. alone. The Bubonic Plague made the War to end all Wars a walk in the park. Eighteen months after the disease appeared, the flu bug vanished and has never shown up again. People wanted to know what happened.

It turns out that while conducting autopsies in 1918, Army doctors had preserved some specimens in formaldehyde. One of these jars contained the lungs of a 21-year-old soldier that died during the pandemic. In 1998, U.S. Army researchers discovered these remains and spent two years extracting seven percent of the genetic code, which provided them with a wealth of information. It appears that the virus passed from birds to pigs, to humans. When the pig's immune system kicks into action, the virus is forced to mutate to survive.

In 1957, the year I was born, we saw it with the Asian flu, ten years later the Hong Kong flu of "68," hit, yet neither of which were as deadly as the 1918 flu. The kicker is - they all came from birds – to pigs – to humans. The scary part is that it could happen again - and we're not prepared for it. Think about the "Bird Flu" talk a few years back.

This country, in its brief history, has seen a lot of war and pain. We have been through two World Wars and perhaps heading to a third World War with this global war on terror - remember 911, and Iran's pursuit of nuclear weapons. That says nothing about the floods, tornados, devastating earthquakes, and the massive hurricanes that have struck our land in recent years. With the onslaught of incurable diseases as Aids, HIV, and the possibility of another "Bird Flu" pandemic, it's a wonder we have any hope for the future. Nevertheless, physical death in the wake of impending danger is the least of our worries. We are in a war that will affect our eternal destination.

Within our borders, a bomb has gone off, more subtle than anything man cooks up. That bomb is the cult and occult explosion. In the previous chapters on Healing of the demonic, I shared how God delivered my family from satan's grip. But there is more to the story. Just to refresh your minds. In my family, the door opened up to the occult world a hundred and thirty years before the current mysticism movement. We were bound by the cult of spiritism, and stayed bound for generations, until the Lord drew a line in the sand.

My great grandmother was a medium when the spiritism revival first took place in the 1880's, but it was not until 1930 when great grandmother made a visit to Grandpa's humble home, in San Diego, that communication with the dead became a reality in Gramps life.

According to my father, Gramps was not too sure about spirit communication. He knew his mother was a devout spiritualist, but it was too hard for him to believe that the spirit world could communicate, let alone communicate through a wooden table. As the story goes, that night, his whole outlook changed. They all gathered around the kitchen table. This table was made of solid oak, weighing a good 300 pounds, and Gramps knew that no "hocus-pocus" from his mother could make that table move. Sitting around the table, everyone would place their fingertips lightly on the face of

the table. Great Grandmother would close her eyes and con-
centrate on some loved one from the past. The intensity of
her trance caused the blood veins on her forehead to stand
out.

The room got quiet, and silence is loud. The only sound
heard was the sound of rapid heartbeats, the kind that
comes in an hour of fear and uncertainty. Suddenly, a chill
filled the air, an unearthly chill that ran down my Grandfather's arms.

"Somebody's trying to get through," Said Great Grandmother, as the table started to shiver.

"I don't believe this!" Grandpa shouted.

Suddenly, the table reared up on two legs, and came slam-
ming down, sliding my grandfather into the corner of the
kitchen. Grandpa's heart was in his throat, pumping uncontrollably, as the table pinned him against the wall.

This started the beginning of my family's involvement in
spiritism. For years, this kind of activity, gaining information
from the world beyond, and seeking relationship with un-
seen entities, plagued my Dad's side of the family. This was
my religion - communication with the so-called spirit world.
This was my history.

I was fourteen, when we moved to Mission Viejo, one of California's most beautiful communities. Located on the south
end of Orange County, this suburban hideaway was surrounded by waves of rolling hills. In the autumn, the hills
came alive with the colors of fall. With the tall grasses blow-

ing in the wind, it was as if a magical hand was orchestrating the movement of the golden hills. I loved those rolling hills, but it was not long before all the hills were whipped away and replaced by more houses, Spanish style homes as far as the eyes could see.

The building of that area exploded as the crowded and radical conditions of Los Angeles pushed people southward. It was as if people were running - trying to find their Utopia, and Utopia it appeared to be. Nevertheless, my folks learned fast that things are not always, as they seem to be.

That was the year I discovered a new playmate and drugs became my best friend. My high school years were marked by extreme rebellion caused by my hippy-fied way of thinking. The high school administration officials had labeled me incorrigible and transferred me to Silverado Continuation School during my sophomore year. At the end of that school year, I dropped out. By the time, I was eighteen I was a wreck. It did not take long for the effects of my torn life style to hurt everything and everyone.

I grew up in a family, struggling with alcoholism, drug abuse, spiritism, and divorce. My parents, though loving, did not know the Lord and their search to fill the void within them lead to many dead ends. The only spiritual influence I had come from spiritism, table moving, and communication with the dead, except for one thing, the touch of one couple in my life as a child.

I had a Bible believing Aunt and Uncle who lived with us when I was a kid. My Aunt Ida Bell and Uncle Harold were strong Christians and had tremendous faith. They never preached at us but I knew that their life was real. My Aunt was in the choir and had a voice of an angel. On a day, I will never forget, I heard for the first time about Jesus – in a personal way. It happened in front of my house in Huntington Beach, California. I was ten years old. I really liked to talk to my Uncle Harold. He was a peaceful man. He worked the produce section at Vons market and he loved his cigars – they were his quiet time.

Early one evening I saw my Uncle standing on the porch smoking a cigar staring out at the sunset. I walked over to him and started asking him questions about school and stuff. His mind was somewhere else. It was dusk and he was staring off into the distant skies. I asked him what he was doing. He looked down at me and with a big smile on his face said, "One day – Jesus is going to come back and his glory will fill the skies," as he pointed to dusk colored orange skies above us. That was the first time I heard about Jesus in a personal way. I never forgot that day. My Uncle, shortly thereafter, became terminally ill and died that same year. I know that the prayers of my Aunt and Uncle were instrumental in my future salvation.

By 1977 I was a lost, drug infested, longhaired beach bum hippy, living on the beach in Huntington, California. That summer, I bumped into a young catholic girl, by the name of Jan, in a bar on the peer in Huntington Beach. She was a good Midwest girl from Michigan. We spent the whole summer together sleeping on the beach and riding my motorcycle around Southern California. She was on school break from Western Michigan. I was a high school dropout and a cook.

We were polar opposites. Nevertheless, we fell madly in love. At summer's end, she told me she had to go back to school. She said goodbye, thinking she would never see me again. However, to her surprise, a month later, I bought a '66 VW bus, drove to Kalamazoo, and showed up at her dorm room door. She hid me in her dorm room until we could find a place to live off campus. We married on July 1 the following year. I had fallen head over heels for her. For the first time in my life, I let down the walls of my heart to love someone, and in return, let them love me. This experience of being loved and loving someone was the door that God used to soften my heart, and move into my life.

On our honeymoon, many strange things started to happen to me. I found myself struggling with emotions that I never felt before. We were on our way to Travis City in Michigan when I found myself thinking about the existence of God a lot. Everywhere we would go the question of God's existence haunted me. We would drive our old blue and white '66 VW Bus by old country and gothic style churches and I would pull over to the side of the road and take a picture. My wife thought I was nuts. I found myself in debates with people, arguing in favor of Jesus Christ. Though I hadn't, yet known Him, the reality of His existence was becoming clear – something inside was being stirred.

We went back to California for Christmas in 78. One debate took place on Christmas Eve. It was a lively debate with my sister about the existence of God. If you knew my sister, and me, this was a common practice. Everyone finally left the table, due to my stubbornness. With a warm beer in my hand and a dazed look on my face, I sat back at the kitchen table, alone and feeling lonelier. I thought about this day, Christmas, a day that was supposed to be religious, but all we did, as a family, was drink and argue. I pushed my beer aside and left for my room disgusted.

As I lay on my bed, staring up at the ceiling, all I could think about was the reality of God. "Are you real?" I thought. Then sleep caught up with me and I was out like a light. That night was the most incredible night I have ever experienced. I had fallen asleep and dreamed a dream that would change my life forever.

In this dream, I was sitting in my bed and suddenly the room filled with radiant blue and white light. Standing in front of me was Jesus Christ. He had His arms outstretched, as if he wanted to hold me, His whole being radiated with heavenly brilliance. He was beckoning me, calling me. I felt His love drawing me, warmth I never felt before - as if He wanted to hold me, enfold me, and comfort me. I knew that this was the Lord. It was as if He could see right through me, as if he knew all my pain, the deep pain, way inside, that hidden child filled with fear and disbelief.

I woke in amazement and told my family about the dream. My sister said, "Who do you think you are some kind of prophet?" I walked away, wondering about this Jesus. For the next few days, all I could think about was this dream. My life suddenly had no meaning – confusion set in and I began to fall apart. The struggle inside me was mounting. The forces of rage and sin began to flare up within me. I did not know where to go for help.

I went to my Aunt's house to have a séance and find out more about the strange dream that I had. That night the table went wild and towards the close of the night, the table was moving at my touch. This was one of satan's last attempts to pull me all the way into his grip. My Aunt was a powerful medium, she would barely touch a table, and the so-called spirits would be summoned. I always wanted to do that, to be just like her, there seemed to be so much power in it.

My Aunt left the room and went into the kitchen to wash the dishes. I was left at the séance table with my wife Jan and Wendy, a friend of ours. I put my fingertips on the table, closed my eyes, and said, "Come to us now." All of a sudden, the table began to move, sliding in circles to each one of us. I looked up with a blank composure and noticed my wife, startled by what had happened dropping her hands from the table. Then Wendy dropped her hands and I was left solo with the table, moving in circles, slowly... then faster, and faster.

My wife shouted, "Fred you're moving the table." With that, I threw my hands in the air and the table stopped. For the first time in my life, I could move the table by myself. "What did this mean?" I thought to myself. "What does this have to do with the dream I had?" These questions were flying through my mind. I went back home, confused by the nights' events.

Soon I began a downward spiral. By January 15, 1979, I was a complete mess again. We were having a party that night. Towards the end of the party, about 3:00 am, I asked my friends if they wanted to have a séance. Everyone agreed, so

I took the table and placed it on top of another table - and within minutes, I was out.

When I came to the room was in a shambles, the table was broken, and my wife was crying. My brother in-law had called the police and my wife cried out, "Get out of here I never want to see you again!"

demonic rage took hold of me. I had tossed furniture around, beaten up my best friend, and threaten everyone in the room. My wife had left me. I found myself running, scared, and alone. I returned to our apartment at Walled Lake and sat on the floor, my mind racing with thoughts of suicidal depression. The pain was bad I wanted to die. The only person I had ever loved was leaving me and the thought of being alone was too unbearable. When suddenly, the dream I had on Christmas Eve was right before my eyes.

In a vision, the Lord was standing before me as before. I looked up to heaven and cried. These words began to form in my mind, "If you're really real, I need you, help me, please help me!" I opened my mouth and got to the "I" in "if" when the presence of the Lord filled the room with warmth like the warmth in my dream. My hair was standing up on end. All I could do was cry. I kept saying repeatedly, "Your real, you're really real!"

The Lord had entered my room and wrapped His arms around me. He took away all my pain, hurt, and sin into Himself and I was, for the first time in my life, forgiven. I was instantly aware that the Lord - He is God! That Jesus loved me, and that He knew me better than I knew myself. I was born again and filled with his Spirit that very minute. Something had happened to me. My eyes were opened for the first time. The demons that bound me were gone. Jesus had set me free. I could see, feel, and hear life for the first time. I knew he had forgiven me of all my sins and I was clean – as white as freshly fallen snow.

My wife had come by the house to pack some clothes and leave. She saw me sitting on the floor and walked right on by. I didn't know how to explain to her what had happened to me. I felt like John Denver in that movie "Oh God." I walked up to her and told her that Jesus came to me... He did something to me. I didn't know how to explain it. I said it would never happen again. Then, by a miracle, she looked at me and forgave me.

That next morning I went to her folk's house. I was sitting in their living room next to a coffee table where they had a big white catholic bible with a picture of Jesus on it. I looked at that picture and tears started to roll down my face. I felt the presence of the Lord all around me, comforting me. I grabbed the bible, opened it, and began to read where my finger hit the page. I read for the first time in my entire life, these words:

> *"For God so loved the world, that he gave his only begotten Son, that whosoever believeth in him should not perish, but have everlasting life. "*

> - John 3:16

The tears began to flow again and the Lord spoke to me,

> *"Fred - I did it for you!"*

I love the Lord so much for that - I love Him more than I can say with words. A few weeks later God was calling us back to my home, to California. On our way back to California, we stopped in a hotel. In the room, they had a Gideon Bible. I began reading it for the first time. I took it with me and held onto it - shoot, I didn't know where to buy one of those things.

Daily I devoured the word. When I read it, the words became alive. The Lord would speak to me, saying, "Fred I have called you to be a prophet to my people, to be a light in a dark place, and a fire before my throne." I did not know what that meant. It was later that I discovered the depth of that call. Of course, we are all called to be witnesses of the resurrected Lord, to be the extension of His hands, to be His voice in a world that is hungry to taste the manna that came down from heaven.

It took me six months to learn what church was all about. I just didn't think in terms like as church and fellowship. All I knew was that Jesus loved me. Daily the Lord would speak to me with that small still inner voice I have come to know and love. At night, I would have the most incredible dreams. We talked, as a friend would speak to a friend. I would see visions and feel his presence daily.

Christian radio was my church for about six months. It did not take the Lord long to bring me into fellowship. It was there that I discovered that many Christians didn't believe that God spoke to His people. I was shocked to find that life in many churches was far removed from what I read in the Scriptures, until I met John Wimber.

My first church was Calvary Chapel in Costa Mesa, under Pastor Chuck Smith. I was immersed in the word. With teachers like Chuck Missler, in depth bible study and worship became my passion. Calvary was the perfect place for being grounded in the word.

That was also the season Bob Dylan was saved. Bob was a hero of mine and when he had been saved I thought, yes God. It blew my mind. It happened at the first Vineyard Church started when Kenn Gulliksen who had brought together two Bible studies groups meeting at the houses of singer/songwriters: Larry Norman and Chuck Girard. This was "Vineyard" before the Wimber years. Bob cut three Christian albums in those years, and they were powerful, "Slow train coming" – "saved" - and "shot of love." Well, in my life, I was experiencing so many manifestations of the Holy Spirit in my life, visions, dreams, hearing God, and being filled with the Holy Spirit were just normal. I had no idea that this activity wasn't fully embraced by Calvary or the church in general at that time. I thought – "it's in the book, surely, everyone experiences God like this."

Shortly after that, God was calling us back to Huntington Beach, but I didn't know it, not until Canadian Immigration detained us. You see we did not have work visas, and many folks had split to Canada during the Vietnam War, so Canadian Immigration was cracking down on immigrants. They were tightening up before amnesty kicked in I suppose. You could say I was a snow-back.... But we were just a couple of young hippies and thought that this was par for the course. We didn't even think we needed visas, after all it was Cana-

da, and my cousin lived there and was married to a Canadian.

I was doing a banquet for some folks. It turned out that their
guest speaker was head of Canadian Immigration. I looked
outside in the snow and saw all these undercover cop cars. I
thought, wow – a lot of cop cars out there. Moments later,
the doors burst open and we were headed down the mountain and placed in immigration holding until we went before
the magistrate. Ironically, I was placed in a cell with a man
who was from a communist bloc country. He had jumped
from a Russian ship and swam to the east coast of Canada,
then hitchhiked across the country, ending up in Vancouver.
I shared with him the love and power of Jesus and He was
saved in that cell.

We soon found ourselves back at home, in Huntington
Beach. I was back at Calvary. By this time in my life, though I
had only been saved for a merely two plus years, I knew I
needed more. It was 1981. That's when I discovered John
Wimber at the Canyon High School in Yorba Linda. When I
arrived it was shortly after that landmark day in Vineyard
history – when on Mother's day, John Wimber asked Lonnie
Frisbee to preach and at the end of his message he called all
the kids under the age of 25 to come forward and hundreds
came up – then he prayed "Come Holy Spirit" and the rest
was history. God just fell on the place. That grace filled
Mother's Day, was the beginning of the future Vineyard
movement.

I found my home. I would spend half my time at Calvary Costa Mesa, learning the word, and half my time at John

Wimber's church, just loving Jesus, worshiping, and soaking in the presence. They were meeting at the old Canyon High School in Anaheim Hills, worshiping on bleachers and seeking the face of Jesus. Then, in 1982, Calvary Chapel of Yorba Linda became the Anaheim Vineyard Christian Fellowship.

After a short season back in the OC, God called us up to Twin Peaks, outside Lake Arrowhead, up in the mountains. A month earlier revival had broken out at the Calvary Chapel Conference Center. God had placed Jan and I right up the hill from the center. Chuck Smith had introduced Lonnie Frisbee at a retreat. I believe Calvary Chapel Yorba Linda was there, and the Holy Spirit fell on that place. Young people all over the place were slain with the Holy Spirit. A home group sprung up around that. Some 50 or so people just hung out in an "A-frame" house, praying and seeking God... and God showed up. Folks were hanging on the balcony, lying on the floor, all with one thing in common, a passion for the Lord and His presence.

Well, our hope was to find a church like Wimber's. We were very excited to find Calvary Chapel Conference Center in Twin Peaks. Combined with the trees and the serenity of the mountains this was a perfect place to move into a deeper relationship with the Spirit of God. The revival that had broken out was still alive, active, and new. It changed the mountain and the atmosphere of church. It was truly electrifying. Many amazing things happened on that mountain, some of which I shared in this series.

After about a year, we left Lake Arrowhead and moved to Palm Springs, a desert community south of Lake Arrowhead. We began attending Calvary of Palm Springs.

By this time, Yorba Linda was now Vineyard Anaheim. I would split my time at Calvary and then drive from Palm Springs to Anaheim Vineyard. Vineyard was alive with the presence of God. You would simply walk in and the presence of the Holy Spirit was upon you.

- Folks were getting healed left and right
- The demonized were being set free everywhere
- Miracles, signs and wonders were part of this new vibrant body of believers
- The worship was alive with the breath of God
- Kinship groups were training camps of fellowship were folks learned to practice the gifts of the Kingdom

The non-pretentious, un-religious message and nature of John Wimber was refreshing for so many of us. We just wanted God to be God. I would try to take folks from Palm Springs with me, so they could experience what I was experiencing. One couple I took was from the Church of Christ. They didn't even believe in instruments being used in the church. Here they were, in a Holy Spirit infused atmosphere of presence and worship, when a young lady in front of us manifested a demon and a ministry team began dealing with that critter. The wife, of my friend, saw that, jumped to her feet and ran out of the church.

Then a new Vineyard plant happened, and Vineyard of Palm Desert was born. I had a new home. Now my Anaheim visits were shorter, maybe once a quarter, and for every conference, "Power Healing," "Power Evangelism," and "Signs & Wonders and Church Growth."

John had a passion and a mission to train, equip, and deploy, and he had a vision to take the message of "doing the stuff" and "everyone gets to play" to world. This naturally supernatural message was affecting denominations around the world.

Like Lonnie Frisbee before him, John was on fire for a personal relationship with the power and presence of Jesus Christ. John put into words everything I believed and was experiencing in my life. His passion for Jesus and his emphases on Christians being authentic, filled, and "doing the stuff," was exactly what my spiritual DNA was crying out for. John Wimber developed a model of ministry that he had dubbed "naturally supernatural" and it reinforced in my heart the Lord's desire to live from a kingdom mindset. His model took ministry off the platform and allowed all of us to participate in lending a hand to "what the Father was doing."

John Wimber was a professional musician who played the Las Vegas circuit for 5 years. John later signed with the Righteous Brothers. When John was gripped by God in 1963, he was a "beer-guzzling, drug abusing pop musician, who was converted at the age of 29 while chain-smoking his way through a Quaker-led Bible Study. One of my favorite stories of John's was when he recalled his first years as a believer. He became a voracious Bible reader and after weeks of reading about life changing miracles in the Bible and attending, what he called "boring" church services. John asked a lay leader at that "boring" church:

"When do we get to do the stuff? You know, the stuff here in the Bible; the stuff Jesus did, like healing the sick, raising the dead, healing the blind – stuff like that?"

He was told that they didn't do that anymore – only what they did in their weekly services. John replied, "You mean I gave up drugs for that?" John used to always emphases, "Everyone gets to play," which meant that all of us could participate in "doin' the stuff." It wasn't just for the pastors and preachers; it was for folks in the pews, folks like you and me. We soon learned that the "real meat was in the street" and Jesus was about to send all out and spawn a church growth movement that was simply remarkable. Everyone being allowed to do the stuff, the emphases on worship, and fellowship through "kinship" groups became part of the guiding foundation, hallmark, and marching orders of the Vineyard Movement in the early years. When I look back at some of the highlight of those years, I yearn for the fundamentals of the early Vineyard, to flood through the Vineyard of today.

- Sold out relentless worship, passion for Christ, and doin' the stuff – 80s – 90s
- Equipping the Saints and kinship empowerment – 80s onward
- Church planting & VMI – 83 onward
- Power healing – 84 onward
- Power evangelism – 85 onward
- Signs, Wonders and Church Growth – 85 onward
- The prophetic – 86 through the 92

John taught me that the most important thing in my life was intimacy with Jesus. That single core value has been my guiding pursuit for much of my Christian walk. I can say with full conviction that John was my true father in the faith, thank you John!

For the next 30 years, the Lord moved my family all around the country and every transition were filled with ecstasy, or pain, or both. It seemed that everywhere we went, we always ended up at a recently planted Vineyard. We would be there for a season – then the wind would blow and off we were again to another location. For me going to church was a treat, a special gift. The life of a chef allows very little time to meet the schedule of church attendance. Weekends, and holidays are our busiest times, so we fit it in where we can.

We would find ourselves living in Milwaukee, Florida, Virginia at the Virginia Beach Vineyard with Todd Hunter during my CBN years with Pat Robertson, Texas, Minnesota, Las Vegas, San Diego and Orlando. In 2003 I ended up on the Gulf Coast of Florida at a resort in the farming community of Ruskin. This pristine coast would be our new home until we came to DC.

Thanksgiving week, 2004 I got a surprise knock on the door. When I opened it, it was my son Jamisen asking if he could stay with us. I was so excited; I turned our living room into a bedroom and got him a job in the kitchen at our resort. Jamisen broke-up with his girlfriend and was devastated. He said, "Dad, I need to come back to the Lord – would you pray with me." We walked down to the dock, below our house. I told him the story of the prodigal, how the father loved his son so much that he leaped off his porch and came running to his son while he was still far off. He put rings on his fingers, shoes on his feet, and a robe on his back – then he threw him a killer party, fatted calf and all. We sat, cried, and prayed together. I had gotten my son back. What I didn't know was in just a few short months, on January 19, 2005, he would be killed.

The great sadness entered in my life. My boy was gone. He was struck in the back of the head by a bullet when a gun accidently went off. The following months, to help in my grief, I wrote a book called "Reflections from the Kitchen, a look at Christ through the Eyes of a Chef." The folks in my kitchen helped Jan and I walk through our grief. However, the sadness never really goes away.

We didn't have a church in that area. It was very rural. Then a funny thing began to happen. The girls in the kitchen kept coming to my office for prayer. Usually it was for healing or for mending relationship – and you know what? God started answering their prayers. People were being healed. Most of my culinary team was Spanish and my Spanish is what you call "kitchen Spanish." What started with two Marias and Rosa soon became 20 people, praying daily in the employee cafeteria.

I was blown away when I started to pray for our Poppa, our King to stand in our midst, using broken Spanish and sign language, and I would look around at our group and people were just weeping. Rodney, a new cook, with a biker headband and tats, walked by the cafeteria and stood frozen at the door, tears streaming down his face. He turned and ran away. I walked back to the fry station to talk to him. "Are you ok?"

He looked at me and said, "That was the most beautiful thing I have ever seen." He asked me to pray for him. We left the kitchen and walked down to the pier and God just came up-on him.

This thing was getting big. By now, my cooks were bringing family members to my office. "Con usted permiso jefe, mi moma..." I would look over and see a little old Spanish lady standing there who needed prayer because she couldn't walk well... And God healed her.

I said, "God this is crazy, what should I do?" So I started "Cooks for Christ" and began having weekly meetings in our banquet room. I bought cases of Spanish/English bibles and began handing them out. By Christmas of that year, at our first 2006 Cooks for Christmas Party, we had 150 people, families, kids, teenagers, and grandparents. Previously I shared the story of Salendra, which occurred during this season in my life.

You see, what I learned about the moving of God's presence, visions, dreams, and the prophetic, was born out of relation-ship with Jesus. It came from a God who said, "I no longer call you my servants but friends." It was birthed in the living room of a dying young man, whom the Lord decided to visit one day. Upon that visitation, there arose a friendship, not that I loved Him, but that He first loved me; and a friend like that is truly worthy of all that we can offer him, namely - our lives.

For decades, satan had bound my family with lying revelation. Yet, I have seen the Son of God turn the table on this deceiver and over the years usher many within my family to the knowledge of His saving grace. The Lord saved my Dad at age 65 and healed our relationship at Vineyard's Healing 86 Conference. My mother received salvation on her deathbed while dying in my arms from cancer as I read to her Psalms 23. My older brother Bob was saved as a teenager. His salvation sustained him while his body was being ravaged by terminal illness. My sister Jean and her husband Greg were saved by observing Christ move in the lives of their children, Chase and Andrea. They were saved as teenagers while staying with us one summer.

My Aunt Eva, former spiritist, was saved after the Lord gave me the opportunity to witness to my Dad's entire side of the family. I had confronted my Aunt about the dangers of table moving, some two years after I was saved. Jesus set her free, and she never picked up or participated in a séance since. Her compassion, faith, and belief in Christ's ability to sustain me were an inspiration. I saw God save my cousin Jim at Vineyard's Power Evangelism conference in 1985, and walk with him while he struggled with cancer. I watched as Jesus wrapped His arms around all of us when my son went to be with the Lord after a terminal head wound. I have seen the renunciation of seeking false revelation, and the love of Christ filled that void in my own life.

I have heard the whisper of the Spirit within my ear wooing me to Him who sits upon the throne. No channeler, no séance, no crystal, or any other lying wonder can stand next to the revelation of Jesus Christ - our true hope! You can be as close to God as you want to be, just let Him in and believe He rewards those who diligently seek Him.

I pray that this book has blessed you in your relationship with Jesus Christ and has equipped you to be more effective in your service to the world.

Embrace your call and bring it to the streets...

Bibliography

Jim Driscoll, The Modern Seer, 2010, Orbital Book Group, 1st Ed.

John Wimber, Keven Springer, Power Healing, 1987, Harper Collins, 1st Ed.

Kris Vallotton, Developing a Supernatural Lifestyle, 2007, Destiny Image, 1st Ed.

Jonathan Welton, The School of the Seer, 2009, Destiny Image, 1st Ed.

Dennis Cramer, Breaking Curses, 1997, Arrow Publications, 1st Ed.

Bill Johnson,

> Release the Power of Jesus, 2009, Destiny Image, 1st Ed.

> When Heaven Invades Earth, 2003, Treasure House, 1st Ed.

Randy Clark, Ministry Training Manual, 2004, Global Awakening, 1st Ed.

About the Author

Fred Raynaud, CEC, CCA – is an Author, speaker, and Chef by
trade. He serves as the Founder and President of CELI (Culinary
Executive Leadership Institute) and the Founder of the
Dreamweaver Outreach program, a street ministry bringing God's
touch to the streets.

For more information please visit our website at
http://www.SeersGift.com

Made in the USA
Columbia, SC
10 June 2018